Cambridge Elements

Elements in Rethinking Byzantium
edited by
Leonora Neville
University of Wisconsin-Madison
Darlene Brooks Hedstrom
Brandeis University

BYZANTINE LAW

The Law of the Eastern Roman Empire

Daphne Penna
University of Groningen
and
KU Leuven

Shaftesbury Road, Cambridge CB2 8EA, United Kingdom

One Liberty Plaza, 20th Floor, New York, NY 10006, USA

477 Williamstown Road, Port Melbourne, VIC 3207, Australia

314–321, 3rd Floor, Plot 3, Splendor Forum, Jasola District Centre, New Delhi – 110025, India

103 Penang Road, #05–06/07, Visioncrest Commercial, Singapore 238467

Cambridge University Press is part of Cambridge University Press & Assessment, a department of the University of Cambridge.

We share the University's mission to contribute to society through the pursuit of education, learning and research at the highest international levels of excellence.

www.cambridge.org
Information on this title: www.cambridge.org/9781009696067

DOI: 10.1017/9781009696074

© Daphne Penna 2026

This publication is in copyright. Subject to statutory exception and to the provisions of relevant collective licensing agreements, no reproduction of any part may take place without the written permission of Cambridge University Press & Assessment.

When citing this work, please include a reference to the DOI 10.1017/9781009696074

First published 2026

A catalogue record for this publication is available from the British Library

A Cataloging-in-Publication data record for this Element is available from the Library of Congress

ISBN 978-1-009-69605-0 Hardback
ISBN 978-1-009-69606-7 Paperback
ISSN 3033-4292 (online)
ISSN 3033-4284 (print)

Cambridge University Press & Assessment has no responsibility for the persistence or accuracy of URLs for external or third-party internet websites referred to in this publication and does not guarantee that any content on such websites is, or will remain, accurate or appropriate.

For EU product safety concerns, contact us at Calle de José Abascal, 56, 1°, 28003 Madrid, Spain, or email eugpsr@cambridge.org

Byzantine Law

The Law of the Eastern Roman Empire

Elements in Rethinking Byzantium

DOI: 10.1017/9781009696074
First published online: January 2026

Daphne Penna
University of Groningen
and
KU Leuven
Author for correspondence: Daphne Penna, d.penna@rug.nl

Abstract: The purpose of this Element is to introduce the study of later Roman law (Byzantine law) to a wider academic audience. Currently a great deal of specialized knowledge is necessary to approach the field of Byzantine law. This Element works to break down the barriers to this fascinating subject by providing a brief, clear introduction to the topic. It makes a scholarly contribution by placing Byzantine law in a broader perspective and by reconsidering some of the aspects of the study of Byzantine law. The Element places Byzantine law outside of the box by comparing, for example, Byzantine law to the European legal tradition and highlighting the role that Byzantine law can have in unravelling the common legal past of Europe. It gives also information on the status of Byzantine legal studies and makes suggestions on how to study Byzantine law and why.

Keywords: Byzantium, medieval history, Roman law, Roman history and culture, canon law

© Daphne Penna 2026
ISBNs: 9781009696050 (HB), 9781009696067 (PB), 9781009696074 (OC)
ISSNs: 3033-4292 (online), 3033-4284 (print)

Contents

Preface	1
1 What Is Byzantine Law, or Does Byzantine Law Exist?	2
1.1 A Question of Terminology	2
1.2 In the Beginning Was Justinian's Legislation	5
1.3 It Is the Language, Stupid, or the 'Birth' of Byzantine Law	8
1.4 From Gaius to Theophilus and Beyond	11
1.5 State Law and Canon Law	14
1.6 Applying the Law	17
1.7 When Does Byzantine Law End, or Does Byzantine Law End?	24
2 How Is Byzantine Law Related to European Law, or Rethinking Byzantine Law	26
2.1 What Have the Romans Ever Done for Us?	26
2.2 It Is the Language, Stupid, or the 'Birth' of European Private Law	27
2.3 What Have the Byzantines Ever Done for Us?	29
2.4 Comparing the Western to the Eastern Legal Tradition	34
2.5 Unravelling the Common Legal Past of Europe	37
2.6 From Harmenopoulos to Windscheid and Beyond	39
2.7 The Future of Byzantine Law	44
List of Abbreviations	48
Bibliography	49

For Winfried, Alexander, and Lydia

Preface

Whenever I say that I am specialized in Byzantine law, most of the people looked surprised, baffled, and occasionally there is a glimpse of pity in their face or even horror. On many occasions in social gatherings, when I am asked what Byzantine law is, it is my beloved husband who takes over the conversation and does his best to answer this question while I sit still and watch him sweating his way through it. The purpose of this Element is to make my husband's life easier, or in other words, the purpose of this Element is to introduce the study of later Roman law (Byzantine law) to a broader academic audience and furthermore, to reconsider some of the aspects of the study of Byzantine law. As far as the language is concerned, I have opted for simple language and have avoided scholarly details.

The Element is divided into two sections. In the first section, I focus on Byzantine law itself. I explain what Byzantine law is, why the sixth-century era of the Roman emperor Justinian is crucial for the 'birth' of Byzantine law, the role of linguistic factors in the evolution of Byzantine law, the 'division' between state and canon laws in Byzantium, the practical applicability of the law in Byzantium and, finally, when or whether Byzantine law ends. In the second section, I study Byzantine law in a broader, comparative perspective and discuss how Byzantine law is related to European law. I try to show why is it important to compare the Western to the Eastern legal tradition and highlight the role that Byzantine law can have in unravelling the common legal past of Europe. I conclude with some thoughts on the recent developments and the future of Byzantine law.

I would like to thank Leonora Neville and Darlene Brooks Hedstrom who trusted me with the completion of this Element and gave me the pleasure of writing it. For indeed writing this Element was a pleasure which let me to synthesize, reconsider, and reflect on my twenty-five years of research on Byzantine law. The Element is thus small, but it encapsulates the research of many years in various topics of Byzantine law, for example, the legal issues that arise between the Italian city states and Byzantium, Byzantine legal commentaries of the eleventh and twelfth centuries, basic Byzantine legislative texts and legal practice, maritime law issues, Byzantine justice, Byzantine legal education, Byzantine law and the humanists, transmission of Byzantine legal sources in the West, and the influence of Roman and Byzantine laws in European legal tradition.

While writing this Element, I looked back with great gratitude to all the historians and colleagues who invited me to collaborate and contribute with my expertise in their research projects. The courses I had the chance to teach in Groningen for many years (i.e. *Seminar Byzantine Law, Codifications in Europe, The Legal Heritage of Europe, Roman Law*) and more recently in Brussels (*Roman Law*), helped me to put Byzantine law in a broader perspective. I would like to thank my colleagues, especially those in Groningen, for trusting me with the teaching of these wonderful courses all these years. The biggest thank you goes to Marios Tantalos, not only for providing comments on the manuscript of this Element, but for all the critical proofreading he has done of various writings of mine the last twelve years or so with great patience and enthusiasm, and for all the discussions, collaborations, and fun we have in our common passion for Byzantine law. Many thanks also to Daan de Vries and the anonymous reviewers of this volume for the useful comments and feedback.

I hope that the reader will enjoy reading the Element and, above all, come to agree with me that Byzantine law is not a boring subject, but rather one with much to offer. I would like to dedicate the Element to my husband, Winfried, for all his strenuous efforts to support Byzantine law and to our two children, Alexander and Lydia, for all the times they had to put up with their parents – mainly my husband – for discussing in front of them all kinds of Byzantine subjects.

1 What Is Byzantine Law, or Does Byzantine Law Exist?

1.1 A Question of Terminology

To begin with, Byzantine law does not exist as such. As with all disciplines and studies that relate to the term 'Byzantium', Byzantine law faces an *a priori* problem of terminology and existence. It is good to realise that the word 'Byzantium' is a conventional term, a term that was used from the sixteenth century onwards to describe the Eastern Roman Empire. The people whom we today refer to as the 'Byzantines' did not call themselves that. They referred to themselves as Romans/*Rhomaioi* ("Ρωμαῖοι") because they were Romans. They called their state 'the Roman Empire' ('βασιλεία τῶν Ῥωμαίων') because this is what their state was: the Roman Empire. Strictly speaking, Byzantine law therefore did not exist – at least not with this name – at the time when it was born.

In fact, I wonder whether we can speak of an actual 'birth' of Byzantine law. Byzantine law, as we will see, did not just appear out of the blue.¹ It was a development, which was to be expected based on the conditions and factors that constituted and formed the Eastern Roman Empire. It was a natural, gradual development of Roman law as it evolved in the Eastern Roman Empire. To put it differently, Roman law was never forgotten in the Eastern Roman Empire. This is again completely logical if we consider that the Byzantines spoke of themselves as Romans because they were Romans. As Bernard Stolte has beautifully phrased it: 'If a *Rhomaios* does not live according to Roman law, who does?'²

As in other fields that deal with the history of the Eastern Roman Empire, the name 'Byzantine' has occasionally created misunderstandings, or it has led to the devaluation of the discipline in question – in our case the law of the Eastern Roman Empire. Because of the misinterpretation of the word Byzantine and the incorrect link of that word to a theocratic or religious society, Byzantine law is, for example, sometimes erroneously thought to be Church law. Others associate Byzantine law with the Ottoman Empire. Moreover, as in the case of other disciplines which deal with the history of the Eastern Roman Empire, the negativity of the word 'Byzantine', has sometimes created an obstacle for the study of the law of the Eastern Roman Empire.³ There was a time that anything that was associated with Byzantium was not worthy of study. It is somehow ironic that the negativity towards anything Byzantine was promoted by philosophers of the Enlightenment, a movement that was rooted in the classics. I say it is ironic because not only did the Byzantines contribute to preserving the works of Greek authors of classical antiquity but also because their education was and remained, in principle, classical.⁴ The famous French philosopher Voltaire (1694–1778) considered Byzantine history ridiculous, unworthy to study, and characterized it as 'a disgrace to the human mind' ('*l'opprobre de l'esprit humain*').⁵ Another significant French contemporary

---

¹ See Section 1.2.
² Stolte, 'Is Byzantine Law Roman Law?', 111.
³ For recent discussions, see Neville, *Sailing Away from Byzantium toward East Roman History*; Cameron, *Byzantine Matters*; Aschenbrenner and Ransohoff, eds., *The Invention of Byzantium in Early Modern Europe*.
⁴ See, for example, Herrin, *Byzantium, The Surprising Life of a Medieval Empire*, 120. Pupils would study the three literary topics of grammar, rhetoric, and logic, and the four mathematical subjects of arithmetic, geometry, harmonies, and astronomy. See also Kaldellis, *Byzantium Unbound*, 55–74 (chapter 3, 'Byzantium for classicists'), where the author makes a strong case about the irony of dismissing the Eastern Roman Empire when its literati curated the Hellenic classical corpus that has come down to us from Antiquity.
⁵ '*C'est ainsi cependant qu'on a écrit l'Histoire romaine depuis Tacite. Il en est une autre encore plus ridicule: c'est l'Histoire byzantine. Cet indigne recueil ne contient que des déclamations*

author, Montesquieu (1689–1755) in his work about the causes of success and decline of the Roman empire, refers with great dislike to Byzantium and writes: 'The history of the Greek empire – for it is thus that the Roman empire is named for the future – is nothing but the stuff of revolts, treasons and deceits.'[6] The writings of the Enlightenment authors – especially the ones by Montesquieu – were widely read. As a result of that, their opinions about Byzantium were adopted and widespread.

The Byzantine scholar Steven Runciman highlights a reference by the British historian Edward Gibbon (1737–1794) to Napoleon's disregard for Byzantium. In his speech to the Assembly during the Hundred Days, Napoleon begs France not to follow the example of the 'Bas-Empire' and 'become a laughingstock to posterity'.[7] Gibbon was certainly influenced by the opinions of Voltaire and Montesquieu about Byzantine history. In his monumental work *The History of the Decline and Fall of the Roman Empire*, he expresses his absolute dislike for Byzantium on numerous occasions. According to Gibbon, Byzantine history is 'a tedious and uniform tale of weakness and misery' and the Byzantines 'assume and dishonor the names both of Greeks and Romans'.[8] As Runciman notes, this unfair treatment of Byzantium by Gibbon is due to a number of reasons including Gibbon's knowledge of Greek which 'was far less profound than his knowledge of Latin',[9] the fact that few Byzantine sources were available to him, and the ideas on Byzantium that had been developed by other authors, including Voltaire and Montesquieu.[10] Moreover, as Runciman describes, when a historian writes such a monumental work covering many centuries, there will come a moment where the author will find a period which he considers uninteresting and will treat it summarily; Runciman adds: 'Chapter 48 of the Decline and Fall, in which Gibbon races through five centuries if Byzantine history, is, historically speaking, the weakest section of the whole work.'[11]

Fortunately, the prejudice against anything Byzantine has largely changed. In the last thirty years or so, research in Byzantine fields has

---

et des miracles: il est l'opprobre de l'esprit humain, comme l'empire grec était l'opprobre de la terre.' from Voltaire's work, *Le Pyrrhonisme de l'histoire*, 265, from: https://fr.wikisource.org/wiki/Le_Pyrrhonisme_de_l%E2%80%99histoire/%C3%89dition_Garnier/15.

[6] '*L'histoire de l'Empire grec – c'est ainsi que nous nommerons dorénavant l'Empire romain – n'est plus qu'un tissu de révoltes, de séditions et de perfidies*' in Montesquieu, *Considérations sur les causes de la grandeur des Romains et de leur decadence*.

[7] Runciman, 'Gibbon and Byzantium', 107.

[8] E. Gibbon, *History of the Decline and Fall of the Roman Empire*. The citations are from Chapter XLVIII: Succession and Characters of the Greek Emperors. – Part I, retrieved on 22 Feb. 2025 from www.gutenberg.org/files/25717/25717-h/25717-h.htm.

[9] Runciman, 'Gibbon and Byzantium', 103.   [10] Ibid.   [11] Ibid.

advanced substantially, as displayed in the number and variety of Byzantine topics that were presented in the last two international congresses of Byzantine studies (Belgrade, 2016; Venice/Padua, 2022), for example. Yet, as far as Byzantine law is concerned, if we compare it to the work that has been done for the study of the Western sources of law in Europe (critical editions, translations of sources, monographs, etc.), it is fair to say that the study of Byzantine law is still in its infancy.[12] Basic Byzantine legal sources, including those of Byzantine Canon law, remain untranslated or need a new critical edition, while several of these sources still remain unedited and patiently await study.

1.2 In the Beginning Was Justinian's Legislation

So, when does Byzantine law 'begin'? Better said, is there a period in which Roman law started its own course in the Eastern Roman Empire? Is there a particular period in which Roman law 'became' Byzantine law? Modern historians are fond of creating timelines and dividing history into periods. This is undoubtedly practical and helps us to have an overview of the different historical periods, but one must remember that these are timelines established by modern scholars. In some cases, the boundaries and names that we give to a specific period bring misunderstanding or lead a specific period to be unduly neglected. For example, there are scholars who are occupied with roughly the same period but give it different names. For instance, 'late Roman' or 'late antiquity', and 'early Byzantine' all refer to the same era.[13] This means that there is a possibility that more researchers are working on similar material, but they do not know or read each other's work.

While undoubtedly timelines and distinctions help us to have an overview of the history, it is good to realize that *we* are the ones who create these time limits. History is an ongoing process. There is not really a date in which Byzantine law was 'born'. As I mentioned earlier, Byzantine law was the logical, gradual development of Roman law in the Eastern Roman Empire. As we will see further on,[14] Byzantine law was 'born' out of a practical necessity: the need of the people who lived in the Eastern Roman Empire to read legal texts that were issued in a language that they did not understand. This requires some explanation. As

---

[12] For an overview of the research in Byzantine law, see Tantalos, 'The History of Research on Byzantine Law'.

[13] This is roughly the period corresponding to the late third century up to the sixth.

[14] See Section 1.3. *It is the language, stupid, or the 'birth' of Byzantine law.*

is well known, Greek was the dominant language in the Eastern Roman Empire. Yet, in the sixth century, emperor Justinian (482–565) issued massive amounts of legislation in Latin. What did the legislation of Justinian consist of? And why did he publish it then in Latin when most of his subjects were Greek-speaking? In order to understand Byzantine law, we need to take a closer look at his legislation and examine these questions.

Justinian (reigned 527–565) was an ambitious emperor who wanted to restore the Roman Empire in all its glory.[15] To do so he used two means: 'arms and laws'. On the one hand, in the military field, he wanted to reconquer the western part of 'his empire' and he partly succeeded in this plan: during his reign, Italy, part of southern Spain, and North Africa were for a short period reconquered. On the other hand, under his reign the codification of Roman law was achieved, which was to become one of the most influential legal works in history. Justinian was not the first Eastern Roman emperor engaged in codifying the law. In the fifth century, emperor Theodosius II issued the *Theodosian Code* (438 AD) which consisted of all imperial laws dating from 312 to 438 AD. Theodosius had also planned to make a collection of writings of the Roman jurists but left this unfinished. It was Justinian who continued the work of Theodosius. To return to Justinian, that he used both 'arms and laws' (*arma et leges*) to achieve his goals is something that he himself mentions in an introductory law of his:

Constitutio Imperatoriam pr.: aims of Emperor Justinian[16]

| *Imperatoriam maiestatem non solum armis decoratam, sed etiam legibus oportet esse armatam, ut utrumque tempus et bellorum et pacis recte possit gubernari* […] | Imperial majesty should not only be graced with arms but also armed with laws, so that good government may prevail in time of war and peace alike […] |

This is a fragment of the so-called *Constitutio Imperatoriam*, a law by Justinian introducing a part of his legislation. Justinian's legislation consisted of four parts, as follows:

i. The *Code* (*Codex Justinianus repetitae praelectionis*), issued in 534, which included all the imperial laws up to the time of Justinian. This was the second, updated version of a first *Code* by Justinian, which was issued in 529. The second version of the *Code* (in 534) is the

---

[15] There is a recent monograph on Justinian, see Sarris, *Justinian: Emperor, Soldier, Saint*.
[16] The English translation that follows is from Birks and McLeod, *Justinian's Institutes*.

version that is preserved today. Justinian's *Code* is divided into twelve books, presumably in tribute to the earlier Roman *Law of the Twelve Tables*.[17]

ii. The *Digest*, which proved to be very influential for the history of European private law, as we will see. The *Digest* was issued in 533 and consisted of fragments of the writings of the great Roman jurists who had lived mostly in the second and third centuries AD. It consisted of fifty books. Justinian ordered the committee that made it to select the best opinions of the Roman jurists and bring them into one book. The *Digest* encapsulates therefore the best of the Roman jurisprudence. It is a treasure of legal science, a kind of a legal encyclopaedia. To put it simply: it offers a legal solution to practically almost any legal problem that can arise. The Greek name of the *Digest* was *Pandects* ('Πανδέκτης'), a term which signifies the comprehensiveness of this work, as it derives from the Greek word 'πᾶν', which means 'everything' and the Greek word 'δέχομαι', which means 'to receive'; hence, the *Pandects* literally means 'containing everything'. The *Digest* had the force of one constitution which means that it was one law, probably one of the lengthiest laws ever being made.

iii. The *Institutes* or *Elements* issued in 533, was a manual for first-year law students, and it was addressed, as the emperor mentions in its title, to 'young enthusiasts of the laws' (*cupidae legum iuventuti*). Apart from being a law manual for students, the *Institutes* also had the force of a law and enjoyed equal status with the *Digest* and the *Code*.[18]

iv. The *Novels* were the new laws, the imperial laws that were issued after 534, after the promulgation of the second, updated *Code*; their full name was *Novellae post Codicem constitutiones*, meaning the imperial laws after the *Code*. Most of the *Novels* were written in Greek. There is no official collection of the *Novels*. There is a private collection of the *Novels* entitled 'Collection of the 168 Novellae' which consists of most of the *Novels* of Justinian and a few of his immediate successors.

The whole legislative project was supervised by Tribonian who held an office that can be compared to the minister of justice of nowadays. In the introductory laws to the *Codex*, the *Digest*, and the *Institutes* we learn about the committees that drafted up these works. Professors of law at that time were members of all these committees and played a significant role in drafting up the legislation. Theophilus, for example, who taught at

---

[17] The *Law of the Twelve Tables* was the first Roman legal compilation issued in ca. 450 BC.
[18] The *Digest* and the *Institutes* became law on 30 December, in the year AD 533.

the law school of Constantinople, was one of the law professors who had taken part in the drafting of the *Code* (its first version), the *Digest* and the *Institutes*. Dorotheus, who taught at the school of Beirut was a member of the committees that had drafted the *Digest*, the *Code* (second version) and the *Institutes*.

In a later period, the whole of the legislative collection of Justinian was referred to as the *Corpus Iuris Civilis* which literally means 'the body of civil law'. The term *Corpus Iuris Civilis* was used in the title of the first critical edition of the legislation of Justinian that was made in Geneva in 1583 by the French jurist Denis Godefroy (1549–1622). Like many scholars of his era, he used a Latin version of his name: Dionysius Godofredus.

1.3 It Is the Language, Stupid, or the 'Birth' of Byzantine Law

Most of the parts of Justinian's legislation were issued in Latin. The *Codex*, the *Digest*, the *Institutes* were in Latin. Since Greek was the dominant language in the Eastern Roman Empire, it was a problem that most of the legislation of Justinian was promulgated in Latin. Why did then Justinian publish his legislation in Latin? There were two good reasons. The first reason was practical. Most of the writings he codified had been written in Latin. For example, the *Digest*, as mentioned earlier, consisted of fragments of writings of Roman jurists and almost all of them had written in Latin. It was therefore simpler to issue this work in Latin. The second reason was ideological. Justinian wanted to restore the Roman empire. What better way to do that than to publish laws in the original language of the Roman empire?

However, the fact remained that most of the people of Justinian's empire could not understand his legislation. He had created this majestic legislation, of which he was duly proud, but people in his empire could simply not understand it. The following logical step was this: shortly after the promulgation of Justinian's legislation, contemporary jurists started to translate parts of Justinian's legislation in Greek, or summarize it in Greek, or comment upon in Greek. When I speak of 'jurists', I basically refer to the law professors at the time of Justinian: the so-called *antecessors*. The word *antecessor* derives from the military terminology. It literally means 'the man leading the way' and was used to describe the officer who marched ahead of the army to determine whether the ground was safe for advance. The law professor had a similar task too because he 'marched ahead' and opened the path of knowledge to his students – just as any good teacher should do for his or her pupils.

The *antecessors*, that is, the law professors at the time of Justinian had therefore to tackle the language problem. They had to teach (mostly) Latin legislation to (most) Greek-speaking pupils. They developed a special teaching method which was thoroughly studied by Herman Jan Scheltema (1906–1981), Professor of Roman Law at the University of Groningen and founder of the Groningen school of Byzantine law.[19] What can a teacher do when he or she must teach a material that is in another language? The teacher translates it into his or her own language. This is exactly what the *antecessors* did. They started translating and adapting Justinian's Latin legislation in Greek to help the students. In short, the teaching method of the *antecessors* consisted of two stages. In the first phase, they provided a translation of the original Latin text that they had to teach. This translation was called an *index* ('ἴνδιξ') and served as a helpful tool for students introducing them to the teaching material. In the second stage, the *antecessors* would return to the original Latin text, the so-called *rheton* ('ῥητόν'), and would provide comments, mostly of a legal nature but also in some cases of a linguistic sort. These Greek comments on various legal aspects were called *paragraphai* ('παραγραφαί'), meaning 'side writings', because students probably wrote them down in the margins of their copies of the Latin *rheton*.

The transition from Latin into Greek by the *antecessors* during the Justinianic period marks the 'birth' of Byzantine law, as Bernard Stolte has explained.[20] To avoid misunderstanding, I would like to clarify that this does not mean that Greek was not used before the sixth century in legal documents. Modestinus, a Roman jurist of the third century AD had written some works in Greek. In Roman Egypt, most legal documents were written in Greek.[21] However, if we really want to put a date, a borderline as to when Byzantine law begins, it is fair to say that the work of the *antecessors* played a significant role in 'creating' Byzantine law. Simply put, Byzantine law was Roman law but in Greek. At least, this is how it began. It is true that eventually Christianity influenced the development of Byzantine law, but Roman law was present throughout the whole period of the Byzantine empire and even beyond that. Moreover, in

---

[19] Scheltema, *L'enseignement de droit des antécesseurs*. For an overview of the teaching method of the *antecessors* including examples with fragments of their teaching and English translations, see Penna and Meijering, *A Sourcebook on Byzantine Law*, 40–65.
[20] See Stolte, 'Byzantine Law: The Law of the New Rome'; and of the same author, 'The Law of New Rome: Byzantine Law' and 'Is Byzantine Law Roman Law?'
[21] See, for example, Taubenschlag, *The law of Greco-Roman Egypt in the light of the papyri, 332 B.C.–640 A.D.* and Yiftach, 'Law in Graeco-Roman Egypt: Hellenization, Fusion, Romanization'.

many prefaces of Byzantine legal texts, we find reflections to the Roman past, something that served also as a means of imperial propaganda in making a connection, that is, a legitimate unbroken connection to imperial Rome. Rome had always been present in Byzantine legal sources.[22] References, for example, were made to the Roman origins of the laws and Roman titles were consistently used in several Byzantine legal texts even after the sack of Constantinople in 1204.[23] Furthermore, in some fields of Byzantine law, one can see influences of the Hellenistic legal tradition. A characteristic example is the Justinianic Novel 118 (year 543) which regulates intestate succession[24] and adopts a system of classes in hereditary succession based on blood relationship, something that is much closer to the Hellenistic tradition than the Roman rules.

The sixth century was thus crucial for the 'birth' of Byzantine law. Roman law began its own course in the Eastern Roman Empire through the work of the *antecessors* and the transition of the legal texts from Latin into Greek. When you translate, you inevitably interpret. This is what happened with Roman law when it was translated, summarized, or adapted into Greek. The *antecessors* gave their own interpretation to the texts, just as any jurist does. Byzantine law gradually evolved through the centuries and was influenced by multiple factors, including canon law. Already from the fourth century, the Church played a role in regulating legal issues, especially in the field of family law.[25]

As far as the language is concerned, it is worth pointing out that the *antecessors* continued to use the legal jargon in Latin.[26] They translated parts of Justinian's legislation in Greek during their teaching but often they kept the legal terms in Latin. One can see, for example, in the *antecessorian* material the Latin names for the different legal terms; for

---

[22] See Pitsakis, "Η ιστορία τῆς Ῥώμης καὶ τοῦ ῥωμαϊκοῦ δικαίου στὰ βυζαντινὰ καὶ μεταβυζαντινὰ νομικὰ ἐγχειρίδια' and Macrides, 'Perception of the Past in the Twelfth-Century Canonists'.

[23] For example, the relevant references in the *Ponema Nomikon* of Attaleiates (eleventh century), prooimion in *JGR* VII, 415–417; in the *Hexabiblos* (fourteenth century), 1.1.1-8 in Heimbach, *Konstantin Harmenopoulos, Manuale Legum,* 20–24 and in the *Syntagma* by Blastares (fourteenth century) in *RhP* VI, 27–30.

[24] If there is no will, the law will determine who your heirs are. This legal process is called intestate succession and takes place when a person dies without a legally valid will.

[25] On the relation between secular and ecclesiastical laws, see Section 1.5.

[26] In many of his writings, Nicolaas van der Wal has examined the problems related to linguistic issues concerning Byzantine legal texts. See, for example, Van der Wal, 'Les termes techniques grecs dans la langue des juristes byzantins' and 'Die Schreibweise der dem Lateinischen entlehnten Fachworte in der frühbyzantinischen Juristensprache'. See also Troianos, *Η ελληνική νομική γλώσσα. Γένεση και μορφολογική εξέλιξη της νομικής ορολογίας στη ρωμαϊκή Ανατολή.*

instance, '*mandati actionem*'[27] (= action of mandate), '[*actio*] *furti*'[28] (= the action of theft), '*fideicommissariai*'[29] (= fideicommissaries) or '*bona fide*'[30] (= good faith). Sometimes, Latin legal terms were written in Greek letters, for example, 'μόρα' for the Latin '*mora*', meaning 'delay' or 'ἐξστιπουλάτου' for '*ex stipulatu*', meaning 'from a stipulation'.[31] Some legal terms were also written as a combination of Latin and Greek letters. This was done, for example, by adding a Greek ending to the Latin root of a word, making the untranslated Latin word fit within a Greek grammatical sentence; for instance, COMPENSATEUEIN (*compensa* <*re*> + teuein = τεύειν), which means 'to compensate'; PACTEUEIN (pact<um> + teuein = τεύειν), which means 'to make an agreement'; and USUCAPITEUEUEIN (usucapi<o> + teuein = τεύειν), which means 'being in a status of acquisitive prescription'. Sometimes the continued use of Latin was not limited to legal terms but was also used for the names of Roman jurists or for Latin names more generally; for instance, '*Ulpianu*'[32], that is, Ulpian and '*GaïU*', that is, Gaius.[33]

1.4 From Gaius to Theophilus and Beyond

The material that derives from the *antecessorian* teaching is fragmentary. It is preserved in various fragments incorporated in later sources.[34] There is however one fortunate exception. That is the so-called *Paraphrasis Institutionum* by Theophilus. Theophilus was an *antecessor*, a law professor who taught at the law school of Constantinople in the sixth century. He must have been a genuine expert in Justinianic legislation since, as mentioned earlier, he had participated in the committees which had created it.[35] The *Paraphrasis Institutionum*, as its title implies, is a paraphrase: a Greek adaptation of Justinian's Latin *Institutes* with additions by Theophilus. The work gives us a good impression of how the *Institutes*

---

[27] BS 743/13 (scholion 9 CA ad B. 19,1,22 = D. 27,1,22).
[28] BS 623/10 (scholion 2 CA ad B. 13,1,21 = D. 13,6,21).
[29] BS 2837/26 (scholion 1 Pc ad B. 48,3,42 = D. 40,4,42).
[30] BS 164/21 (scholion 8 V ad B. 8,2,99 = C. 2,12,26).
[31] The stipulation (*stipulatio*) was the most important verbal contract in classical Roman law. It consisted of a promise in a form of a question by the creditor and an affirmative answer by the debtor. There were strict formalities that had to be exercised for this verbal contract to be legally valid. On the classical stipulation and its development, see Zimmermann, *The Law of Obligations. Roman Foundations of the Civilian Tradition*, 68–94.
[32] BS 1928/4 (scholion 3 F Pa ad B. 28,8,43 = D. 24,3,45).
[33] BS 927/11 (scholion 2 Π ad B. 16,1,10 = D. 7,1,10).
[34] See, Penna, 'Law Teaching at the Time of Justinian' (Section 1.5. Where Do We Find Antecessorian Writings?).
[35] See the last part of Section 1.2.

were taught by the law professors at that time. Unfortunately, Theophilus' paraphrase of the *Institutes* is the only work by an *antecessor* that we possess in full.[36] There is a recent critical edition of the *Paraphrasis* with an English translation.[37]

The writings of the Roman jurists have also been preserved only in a fragmentary form with one fortunate exception: the *Institutes*, a legal textbook written by the Roman jurist Gaius in the second century AD. It was only in 1816 that that Gaius' *Institutes* were discovered by purely coincidence in a library in Verona by the German scholar Barthold Georg Niebuhr (1776–1831). While he was reading a manuscript containing some of the works of St Jerome, Niebuhr realized that the manuscript was a so-called palimpsest, namely a reused manuscript containing two or more layers of writing.[38] The lower layer of the palimpsest that Niebuhr was studying contained the lost work of Gaius. Having the whole text of the *Institutes* of Gaius at their disposal, scholars were able to compare it to the *Institutes* of Justinian and conclude that the latter is considerably based on the first one.

Hence, Theophilus' *Paraphrasis*, being a Greek adaptation of Justinian's *Institutes* is also indirectly related to the *Institutes* of Gaius. We do not know why only Gaius' *Institutes* have survived from Roman writings and only Theophilus' paraphrase of the *Institutes* from the *antecessorian* writings. It could be pure coincidence. However, both texts have something in common: they are textbooks explaining law in a simple and comprehensible way. In the long history of the transmission of Roman and Byzantine legal texts, the legal texts we possess in full, from the very early times (i.e. the Roman period, second century AD, and the early Byzantine period, sixth century) are both somehow related to teaching. That, I believe, cannot be a coincidence. Further, in the history of the 'transmission' of Gaius' *Institutes* – meaning the transmission from the latter *Institutes* to Justinian's *Institutes* and finally, its paraphrase by Theophilus – there is another text which is somehow related to the above material but stems from a much later period. It is a textbook in Greek entitled the 'Royal Institutes'

---

[36] The *Epitome novellarum* by the *antecessor* Julianus is another fortunate exception but that was written in Latin. As mentioned earlier, the *Novels* were written in Greek. The majority of the students at the time of Justinian spoke Greek but there were a few students who were Latin-speaking. That is why Julianus compiled the so-called *Epitome novellarum* which was a 'short version' of the *Novels* in Latin.

[37] Lokin, Meijering, Stolte, and Van der Wal, *Theophili Antecessoris Paraphrasis Institutionum*.

[38] The word 'palimpsest' derives from the Greek word 'παλίμψηστος', which literally means 'scraped again', and it indicates a manuscript whose surface has been scraped off to prepare it for reuse.

(τὰ Βασιλικὰ Ἰνστιτοῦτα). According to Marios Tantalos, this textbook dates from 1706 and was written by Nikolaos Komnenos Papadopoulos, a Cretan professor at the law school of Padua.[39] Tantalos argues further that Papadopoulos compiled this work after a request of his former student and later the patriarch of Jerusalem, Chrysanthos Notaras (1655/1660–1731). The latter, in turn, used the 'Royal Institutes' as a source for his own textbook, the 'Introduction to the laws' ('Προθεωρία εἰς τοὺς Νόμους').[40] The 'Royal Institutes' is substantially based on Theophilus' paraphrase of the *Institutes*.[41]

The teaching of the *antecessors* did not last very long. Nevertheless, their work had a significant impact in legal thought in Byzantium. This needs some explanation. Justinian had implemented the teaching of his legislation in the new curriculum of legal studies which he introduced in the two law schools of Constantinople and Beirut. In the introductory laws to his legislation, he gives instructions to the *antecessors* on what material (i.e. which part of his legislation) they must teach in every year.[42] The study lasted five years in total. Roughly speaking, the teaching material was divided as follows: in the first year, students were taught mainly the *Institutes*; in the following three years, parts of the *Digest*; and in the last year, the *Code*. The two law schools of Justinian's day did not last very long. The school of Beirut was destroyed in 551 by an earthquake which practically demolished the whole city, whereas the law school in Constantinople presumably ended about the time of Justinian's death. At the end of the sixth century, law was taught by practitioners, the so-called *scholastici*. They were not occupied with the difficult original Latin legal texts but preferred to use the Greek summaries.

Was the antecessorian material forgotten? Certainly not. First, the *scholastici* did use writings of the *antecessors*, in particular summaries in Greek. Second, writings of the *antecessors* got a new lease of life at a later stage, being incorporated into later works. In fact, this is the way these *antecessorian* fragments have been preserved. As mentioned earlier, works of the law professors of Justinian's time have been preserved in their majority only as fragments in later works, in particular, in the *Basilica* and their scholia.[43] Byzantine jurists of the eleventh and twelfth centuries referred to

---

[39] Tantalos, 'Τὰ «Βασιλικὰ Ἰνστιτοῦτα» (1706). Ἕνα ἀθησαύριστο ἔργο τοῦ Νικολάου Κομνηνοῦ Παπαδοπούλου καὶ ἡ διάδοσή του στὸν ἑλληνικὸ χώρο'.
[40] Ibid.
[41] Tantalos and I have started a critical edition of the 'Royal Institutes' with an English translation and commentary.
[42] See in detail, Penna and Meijering, *Sourcebook Byzantine Law*, 34–42 and Penna, 'Law Teaching at the Time of Justinian', 135–138.
[43] On the *Basilica* and their *scholia*, see further on in detail in Section 2.3, 31–33.

antecessorian works and showed their admiration for the law professors of the sixth century.[44] For example, in the *Peira*, a Byzantine source dating from the middle of the eleventh century and consisting of verdicts and statements of the high-court judge Eustatheios Rhomaios, the judge referred to the *antecessors* Stephanus, Theophilus, Cyrillus, and Thalelaeus by name. The *antecessors* were also praised in the West by the legal humanists who also referred to their works. Jacques Cujas (1522–1590), the most eminent of all legal humanists showed his respect and admiration for the *antecessors* by adding the honorific Latin word 'noster' (= our) before the name of Theophilus just as he had done for Accursius.[45] It is true that the teaching of the *antecessors* did not last long but through the transmission of their works over the centuries, they have indeed proved to be worthy of their name by opening the path of knowledge not only to their contemporary students but also to future generations of jurists.

1.5 State Law and Canon Law

Byzantine law does not consist only of Roman law. In Byzantium, there was not a strict separation between the state and the Church and that influenced the legal field as well. For the Byzantines, it was God who had placed the emperor as the head of the state. The emperor's authority derived from God. This explains why it was the emperor who summoned important ecclesiastical synods and why he was so interested in dealing with ecclesiastical matters. The first ecumenical council held in Nicaea in 325 was convened by the Roman emperor Constantine I, who presided over the first session and took part in the discussions. The word 'ecumenical' derives from the Greek word 'oikoumene' (οἰκουμένη) which means 'the inhabited world'. An ecumenical synod therefore is a gathering of bishops from the entire Christian world. Religion was part of the state's affairs, and imperial legislation thus dealt inevitably with religious issues. Obviously, the emperor interfered with ecclesiastical affairs for political reasons since Christianity formed a unifying factor for the people within his empire.[46] The rules of the Church were the canons. The Greek word 'κανών' literally means 'rule', 'measure'. Canon law deals with the rules and norms that regulate the Church. Strictly speaking, canons are the rules

---

[44] For examples, see Penna, 'Law Teaching at the Time of Justinian', 149–150.

[45] Accursius (c. 1182–1263) was an Italian medieval legal jurist who collected the most important medieval comments (*glossae*) in the West on Justinian's codification and compiled the so-called 'Accursian gloss' which became the standard book of applying Roman law in the Middle Ages.

[46] Papagianni '4.2. Canon law and its status in the Byzantine legal system'.

laid down by an ecumenical council. Nevertheless, there can also be other rules, such as those laid down in a local council or by a Church Father if they have been officially accepted and authorized, that is, 'canonized'. For example, the ecumenical synod of 691/92[47] ruled that canons of the local synods and the church fathers, as well as the so-called apostolic canons, were confirmed and thus had canonical status.

What complicates the situation even further is that the Byzantine emperors also issued laws that, to a certain extent, covered the same ground as the church canons. The emperor was not the head of the church, but he had considerable power and his laws about church matters were generally considered as legally valid. However, they are not 'canons' in the strict sense of the word, but rather laws or 'nomoi'.[48] These imperial constitutions issued by Justinian and other emperors are mainly found in the beginning of Justinian's *Code* and *Novels*. For example, the first thirteen titles of the first book of Justinian's *Code* (from the second edition of the *Code*) deal with church issues including dogmatic principles that were settled in the ecumenical councils, issues dealing with ecclesiastical property, clergy, monks, the administration of justice by bishops, heresies, sacraments, and so on. Many Justinianic *Novels* thus refer to ecclesiastical organization and monastic life.

Eastern Roman emperors attempted in some cases to harmonize secular and canon laws. In 531 emperors Valentinian and Marcian ordered in a constitution that all pragmatic sanctions which contradicted the sacred canons and had been obtained through favour or political intrigue were declared null and void.[49] In one of his constitutions dating from 530, Justinian acknowledges that sacred canons have the same validity as secular laws. The emperor mentions that according to the canons, it was forbidden for presbyters, deacons, and subdeacons to marry after their election. He notes, 'Since, then the punishment for this offence consisted in mere loss of priestly office, and *since Our laws desire that the sacred canons possess no less force than the laws, We decree that the provisions of the sacred canons shall apply to them as if they had been written in the civil laws.*'[50]; and further on he adds, 'For as such conduct had been prohibited by the holy canons,

---

[47] This synod, known as the 'Trullan Synod', was convened in the domed hall (=Trullo) of the imperial palace in Constantinople (in the Trullo, hence the name 'Trullan Synod'). It is also known as the 'Quinisextum' synod because it supplements the last two synods, namely the fifth and sixth.
[48] About the relation between state law and canon law, see Troianos, 'The Creation of a Parallel Legal Order: Canon Law'.
[49] Preserved in Justinian's *Code*, see C. 1,2,12,1.
[50] C. 1,3,44,1; English translation from Frier, *The Codex of Justinian: A New Annotated Translation with Parallel Latin and Greek Text*, 119.

so too has it been checked by Our laws; [...] *What the sacred canons forbid, We too prohibit by Our laws...*'[51] Fifteen years later, in one of his *Novels*, Justinian declares that the canons of the four ecumenical councils that have been held by then (in Nicaea, Constantinople, Ephesus, and Chalcedon) have the force of a law:

> Accordingly, *we decree that the holy ecclesiastical canons* issued or confirmed by the four holy councils – to wit, that of the 318 at Nicaea, that of the 150 holy fathers at Constantinople, the first at Ephesus, at which Nestorius was condemned, and that at Chalcedon, by which Eutyches was anathematised together with Nestorius – *are to rank as laws*. We also accept the dogmas of the aforesaid four holy councils, just as we accept the divine scriptures, and we uphold their canons as laws.[52]

This acceptance of one religion's internal decisions as part of Roman law was a striking evolution of both law and the Roman state.

When it comes to state law and canon law in Byzantium, there is a particular form of compilation that must be mentioned, the so-called 'nomocanones'. What were these compilations? The constitutions or 'nomoi' dealing with ecclesiastical issues were at first listed in an appendix to the collections of canons, but later they were integrated within the collections themselves. The result were new collections, the so-called 'nomocanons' (*nomocanones*), which combined canons of ecclesiastical origin (*kanones*) and of secular laws (*nomoi*). The best-known Byzantine *nomocanon* is the one is the *Nomocanon in Fourteen Titles*, which was originally compiled at the beginning of the seventh century but was revised at the end of the ninth century and in the end of the eleventh century as well. Recently there is increased scholarly interest in this neglected Byzantine genre.[53]

In Byzantium there was no clear border of the powers of the emperor and the patriarch. There is however one Byzantine legal text that attempted to regulate the relations between the state and the Church. The *Eisagoge* is a work that dates from the end of the ninth century.[54] The second and third titles of the *Eisagoge* describe the functions of the

---

[51] C. 1,3,44,2 and C. 1,3,44,4.
[52] *Novel* 131 of Justinian in 545. The English translation cited from Miller and Sarris, The Novels of Justinian: Complete Annotated English Translation.
[53] See Morton, *Byzantine Religious Law in Medieval Italy*.
[54] For an overview of all dating issues of this work with all relevant literature, see Van Bochove, 'Some Byzantine Law Books. Introducing the Continuous Debate Concerning Their Status and Their Date'. There is a Spanish translation of the *Eisagoge* by Signes Codoñer and Andrés Santos, *La Introducción al derecho (Eisagoge) del Patriarca Focio*. A new critical edition of the *Eisagoge* with a German commentary is under preparation by Martin Vučetić as part of the research project of editing Byzantine legal works of the Göttingen Academy of Sciences.

emperor and the patriarch and, accordingly, the relationship between the state and the church. The author of these titles claims a position of considerable authority and power for the patriarch. This has led scholars to believe that Photius, who was patriarch of Constantinople in this period, must have had a significant role in the drafting of the *Eisagoge*. Photius (c. 810 died after 893) was a great intellectual in Byzantium and was known for his famous library which consisted of works on many disciplines including theology, history, grammar, philosophy, law, the natural sciences, and medicine. He had a turbulent ecclesiastical career. He served two times as patriarch of Constantinople (from 858 to 867 and from 877 to 886) and he was also two times deposed from this function. The contemporary views on Photius vary. In any case, modern scholars believe that he must have been the author of a substantial part of the *Eisagoge*. To explore the interaction between the state and the Church further, we will turn next to Byzantine legal practice and especially the jurisprudence of ecclesiastical courts.

1.6 Applying the Law

In the field of Byzantine Legal History, one of the basic questions is how law was applied in Byzantium. This question is undoubtedly difficult to answer, mainly due to the lack of the relevant sources. Scholars tend to divide Byzantine legal sources into: (i) sources that reflect 'the law in the books', mainly laws and legal collections and (ii) sources that are related to 'the law in action', or real practice, for example, judicial decisions, texts related to the courtroom, commentaries that deal with legal practice, and so on. There are several Byzantine legal sources that reflect the 'law in books'; these are in principle legislative texts and all texts that derive from them. For example, all parts of Justinian's legislation (*Codex*, *Digest*, *Institutes*, *Novels*), the eighth-century *Ecloga*, legal collections such as the *Rhodian Sea-Law* or the *Farmer's Law*, the legislation of the ninth and tenth centuries (the *Prochiron*, the *Eisagoge*, the *Basilica* and all the works that derive from them), laws of various emperors, legal treatises, and legal compilations, such as the treatise about actions (*De Actionibus*), the *Ponema Nomikon*, and the *Hexabiblos*.[55]

The sources that reflect 'law in action' are rare. These are sources that are directly related to legal practice, such as legal decisions, statements,

---

[55] For the Byzantine legal sources, see Troianos, *Die Quellen des byzantinischen Rechts*. For an overview of basic Byzantine legal sources with examples and English translations, see Penna and Meijering, *A Sourcebook on Byzantine Law*.

and opinions of legal practitioners or commentaries on judicial material. In other words, there are few sources that reflect actual Byzantine legal practice. A fortunate exception is the *Peira* which dates from the middle of the eleventh century. As mentioned earlier,[56] the *Peira* is a collection of verdicts and other statements of the judge Eustathios Rhomaios, who served as a high judge at the imperial court in Constantinople. This text was not composed by judge Rhomaios himself but presumably a pupil or an assistant of Rhomaios who deeply admired the work of this judge and decided to select and publish several of his verdicts and statements.[57] Dieter Simon has remarked that 'there is no way to describe the legal system of the *Peira* because no such system exists. The judge seeks his inspiration not only in the old commentators of the Justinianic legislation, the *antecessores* but also in literary authors, such as Homer.'[58] It is also true that in some cases the judge Rhomaios dismisses the harshness of the written law and moderates the penalties based on his judgment and common sense. The leniency and the moderation of penalties is related to a typical Byzantine concept called 'oikonomia' which could be translated as 'deliberate modification', and in practice meant making an exception to the rule. The term 'oikonomia' appears also in Byzantine ecclesiastical literature and other genres too. When choosing between two penalties, a Byzantine judge would sometimes apply 'oikonomia': he would then choose the less harsh penalty because he believed that this was the most sensible thing to do. Showing mildness, compassion (φιλανθρωπία, i.e. philanthropy) was after all a virtue that a good jurist should have, according to Byzantine authors.[59] As Psellus mentions 'the person who judges is therefore ready to break the law for the sake of compassion (philanthropy)'.[60]

The literary references to Homer or Aristotle by Rhomaios or the leniency that he exhibited in some cases does not mean that Rhomaios did not know and use the laws. On the contrary, in several cases, we observe that Rhomaios both knew the laws and was able to understand and apply

---

[56] See Section 1.4.
[57] There is a critical edition of the *Peira* with a German translation and commentary and elaborate indices by Simon and Reinsch, Ἡ Πεῖρα – *Die Peira. Ein juristisches Lehrbuch des 11. Jahrhunderts aus Konstantinopel – Text, Übersetzung, Kommentar, Glossar*.
[58] Oikonomides, *Peira*, summarizing in English this observation from Simon, *Rechtsfindung am byzantinischen Reichsgericht*.
[59] See Saradi, 'The Byzantine Tribunals: Problems in the Application of Justice and State Policy (Ninth to Twelfth Centuries)', 186–187.
[60] 'ὅ τε γὰρ δικάζων ἕτοιμος καὶ τὸ δίκαιον παραθραῦσαι φιλανθρωπίας γε ἕνεκα'. *Psellus, Epistula* 117, 30–32 in Papaioannou, *Michael Psellus Epistulae*, vol. 1, 272.

concepts of Roman law.[61] Moreover, in his era, his references to literary authors could also be considered an expression of his broad knowledge. Perhaps Rhomaios added the literary references to help his argument, or perhaps they may have simply displayed his knowledge, which would have augmented his prestige and authority. Let us not forget that the author who wrote the *Peira* deeply admired Rhomaios and presumably wanted to show that this judge was indeed a very learned and erudite man. Perhaps in Byzantine jurisprudence, it was not uncommon for judges to add some arguments of broad knowledge and not to stick to the letter of the law. We cannot be sure of this because we do not have enough material to compare and make safe conclusions. In any case, Rhomaios is not the only judge who refers to Homer or Aristotle. In a later period, we observe that the bishops Chomatenos and Apokaukos, who lived in the thirteenth century, judged legal cases and used literary references in their verdicts and statements.[62]

Another source for Byzantine legal practice is the so-called *Ecloga Basilicorum*, which is a selection of the first ten *Basilica* books accompanied by a commentary dated to the middle of the twelfth century, presumably composed around the year 1142.[63] The *Basilica* was a massive legal compilation rendering Justinianic law in Greek and was issued in around 900.[64] The first ten *Basilica* books mainly cover issues related to justice, such as the organization of the courts, jurisdiction matters, and competent courts, advocates, appeals. The commentator offers lengthy comments on these books of the *Basilica*. The *Ecloga Basilicorum* is therefore valuable because it is one of the few works that could give us information about the actual Byzantine legal practice in the twelfth century.[65] The commentator also provides names of contemporary judges and makes references to officials who lived at the time and sometimes also to contemporary political situations.[66] As Ruth Macrides has shown, the commentary of the *Ecloga Basilicorum* allows us to reconstruct the courts of the twelfth century and the rules for their jurisdictions.[67] What seems most plausible is

---

[61] See Sirks, 'The Peira: Roman law in Greek setting' and of the same author 'Peira 45.11, a presumed succession pact, and the Peira as legal source' and 'How legal is the Peira? Cases and problems'. See also Tantalos, 'Forms of Suretyship in the *Peira* in the Light of the *Basilica*'.
[62] See further on in this section.
[63] Critical edition by Burgmann, *Ecloga Basilicorum*.
[64] See in detail about the *Basilica*, in Section 2.3, 29–33.
[65] See Penna, 'A Witness of Byzantine Legal Practice in the Twelfth Century. Some Remarks on the Construction of the *Ecloga Basilicorum*.'
[66] See on this Burgmann, 'Vier Richter des 12. Jahrhunderts' and Macrides, 'The competent court', especially 119 with the relevant references to the *Ecloga Basilicorum*.
[67] Macrides, 'Competent court', especially 119.

that the commentator of the *Ecloga Basilicorum* was someone at home in the courtroom who knew well the legal practice of the day. Most probably, he was a judge himself as in one of his comments he does in fact refer to a judgment in which he had taken part.[68] It is worth noting that in some manuscripts, we find parts of the commentary of the *Ecloga Basilicorum* inserted as comments to a later source the *Hexabiblos*, which was a legal manual compiled by the judge Constantine Harmenopoulos in fourteenth-century Thessaloniki.[69] This proves that the commentary of the *Ecloga Basilicorum* remained useful even for later generations of Byzantine jurists who dealt with legal practice.

Another source that can provide us with some information on legal practice in the middle Byzantine period are the 'new' *Basilica* scholia, which are directly related to the revival of legal activity in Byzantium which took place in the middle of the eleventh century. Around 1045, Ioannes Xiphilinos, an intellectual of that time, was appointed by the emperor as head of the law school in Constantinople. Xiphilinos and other jurists of the eleventh and twelfth centuries, such as Nicaeus and Hagiotheodorites, wrote scholia on the *Basilica*, and these are known as the 'new' *Basilica* scholia.[70] Some of these 'new' *Basilica* scholia reveal a relatively high legal standard. That is certainly the case for Hagiotheodorites. There are many scholia (nearly two hundred) that have been preserved with his name and because they are so extensive, they offer rich and interesting material for reaching conclusions on his legal thought.[71] In short, the material scope of his scholia and his approach altogether show a rather sophisticated level of legal knowledge. Moreover, Hagiotheodorites explained difficult legal problems in a clear way and tried to help students master the material in an efficient but also pleasant way. Other sources that can help us answer the question

---

[68] See Burgmann, *Ecloga Basilicorum*, XVIII and Macrides, 'The competent court', 118.

[69] Matses, 'Τὰ σχόλια εἰς τὴν Ἑξάβιβλον τοῦ Ἁρμενοπούλου καὶ ἡ Ἐκλογή ἐκ τῶν 10 πρώτων βιβλίων τῶν Βασιλικῶν'. Matses has counted 61 *scholia* in the *Hexabiblos* deriving from the *Ecloga Basilicorum*. On the *Hexabiblos*, see Section 2.6.

[70] On these 'new' *Basilica* scholiasts, see my publications: 'Hagiotheodorites: the last antecessor? Some remarks on one of the "new" *Basilica* scholiasts'; 'The Eleventh-Century Byzantine Jurist Nicaeus: His Scholia on the *Basilica* Laws and His Connection to the *Meditatio de nudis*'; 'Of the *nomophylax*: John Xiphilinos' scholia on the *Basilica*' and 'Studying the "new" *Basilica* scholia: a first evaluation'. On the 'old' and 'new' *Basilica* scholia, see Section 2.3.

[71] See, in detail, earlier, the studies about Hagiotheodorites and Penna, 'Hagiotheodorites, once again. A few remarks on two of his *Basilica* scholia'. For the legal argumentation of more Byzantine commentators, see the studies by Paparriga-Artemiades. For example, '*Les scoliastes byzantins face aux ambiguïtés des lois*' and of the same author 'Interventions of the *interpretatio iuris* to the resolving of the ambiguities of law during the byzantine period'.

of the application of law in Byzantium are some imperial documents which are related to legal practice, for example, the *Novel* of Manuel I Komnenos in 1166 on court procedure. Additionally, considerable legal material survives in monastic archives. There are many legal documents that have been preserved in monastic archives: about 1100 medieval legal documents from Mount Athos, as well as a few dozen from other collections, court decisions, contracts of sale or exchange, and so on.[72]

Up to now I have referred to sources from the sphere of secular law and, as mentioned earlier, the only source that includes verdicts of a Byzantine judge is that of the *Peira*. Fortunately, we have more evidence from the decisions of ecclesiastical courts in Byzantium. From the time of emperor Constantine, the Great (ca. 272–337 AD) episcopal jurisdiction (*audientia episcopalis*) was recognized by the state.[73] Christians were allowed to bring their disputes before a bishop. In some cases, ecclesiastical courts were the only competent courts to judge specific cases, such as lawsuits where the parties were clerics. Gradually, ecclesiastical courts received more competences. In the eleventh century, the emperor Alexios I Komnenos issued laws recognizing the authority of the Church in cases of marriage law, donations and bequests for charitable causes and presumably also some cases dealing with slaves.

After the sack of Constantinople in 1204, particular bishops in the Despotate of Epirus also attracted legal cases to their courts due to their knowledge and personality. Such is the case of Demetrios Chomatenos, who served as the archbishop of Ohrid from 1216 to 1236. Scholars believe that Chomatenos must have had a remarkable collection of books because he often cites fragments of the sources he uses.[74] His decisions and statements covered many fields of law, including issues about marriage law, succession, and criminal law. We know this because he published his replies. His collection is entitled 'ponemata diaphora' ('Various works') and consists of around 150 verdicts, letters, and legal opinions.[75] This valuable

---

[72] The vast majority of the monastic documents in Athos have been edited in the series 'Archives de l'Athos'.

[73] On the establishment and the development of the episcopal jurisdiction, see Pantazopoulos, *Church and Law in the Balkan Peninsula during the Ottoman rule*. On the evolution of the division of power in terms of judicial competences between the imperial authority and the Church in Byzantium, from the tenth to the fifteenth centuries, see Goudjil, *Une symphonie des pouvoirs judiciaires à Byzance. Le rôle de l'Église dans l'administration de la justice (Xe–XVe siècle)*.

[74] See also the following text in this section where some conclusions are presented from research done on the jurisprudence of ecclesiastical courts by Eleftheria Papagianni.

[75] Critical edition with introduction and indices by Prinzing, *Demetrios Chomatenos, Ponemata diaphora. Das Aktenkorpus des Ohrider Erzbischofs Demetrios Chomatenos. Einleitung, kritische Edition und Indizes*.

collection gives us a good impression of what kinds of cases were brought before a bishop's court, as well as information on the applicable law and the sources used in this period. The same can be said for the acts of another churchman of this period, Ioannes Apokaukos (born c. 1155, died 1233), who served as a bishop in Naupaktos, a city in present-day western Greece.

What is interesting is that – in line with Rhomaios' practice – both Apokaukos and Chomatenos have references to classical authors from antiquity, such as Homer, Aristotle, and Aristophanes, in their verdicts and statements. Even though both Apokaukos and Chomatenos came from ecclesiastical circles, they did not hesitate to use in their verdicts passages from works of the ancient classics who were in fact considered by the church 'pagan' and 'heretics'. As has been observed by other scholars, 'homo Byzantinus remained true both to his classical learning and his Christian beliefs'.[76] One must take into account that classic authors of antiquity (Aristotle, Plato, Aristophanes, Sophocles, and, above all, Homer to mention a few) had always formed a significant part of Byzantine education. Any learned man was supposed to have read and studied at least selections from classical authors. And by saying any learned man, this included men of ecclesiastical circles.

Despite the efforts of modern historians to present an objective picture of Byzantine civilization,[77] there is still a tendency by some to regard Byzantium as a rather backward, obscure, or even a purely theocratic empire. This tendency is unfair. Byzantine education, and Byzantine jurisprudence, proves the opposite. To put it simply, there was no interruption of classical studies in Byzantium. The Byzantines always studied the works of classical authors including Homer. Let us not forget that we have the classics almost entirely because the Byzantines preserved them. It was the Byzantines who copied Homer and other classics in their manuscripts and studied them. Homer and authors of classical antiquity were part of the curriculum of the secondary level of education, the so-called *enkyklios paideia*.[78] Byzantine education was reflected in Byzantine jurisprudence, judging from the few Byzantine verdicts that we have. In fact, as I have argued in another study, it is probably not coincidental that both the Byzantine judge Rhomaios (eleventh century) and the bishop Apokaukos (thirteenth century) cite the

---

[76] Markopoulos, *Education in Constantinople during the Byzantine period* with reference here to Cavallo, *Lire à Byzance*, 11–21.
[77] See, for example, Herrin, *Byzantium. The Surprising Life of a Medieval Empire* and Cameron, *The Byzantines*.
[78] See, for example, Markopoulos, 'Education in Constantinople during the Byzantine period' and of the same author 'Education'.

same Homeric fragment in two of their verdicts. They cite the Odyssey where the goddess Athena tries to convince Telemachus to return to Ithaca before his mother gets remarried and refers to the nature of women.[79] My hypothesis is that this specific fragment was part of the standard Homeric excerpts that pupils had to study in their curriculum. Furthermore, Apokaukos also refers also to works of Aristophanes in his statements and verdicts and I do not think he does so to strengthen his legal arguments. My impression is that Apokaukos cites Aristophanes either to show off his knowledge, or more likely, to ridicule a particular situation. He is citing the great comic playwright because it is funny. Those who harbour negative stereotypes about Byzantium being a theocratic and decadent society may be rather surprised to see that a Byzantine bishop uses Aristophanes in his verdicts to have some fun.[80]

Several verdicts have also been preserved from the patriarchal court of Constantinople from the fourteenth century.[81] Eleutheria Papagianni has studied the Byzantine ecclesiastical jurisprudence exhaustively and has published several studies on this subject including three extensive volumes which deal with cases in the Byzantine ecclesiastical courts from the eleventh century up to 1835 regarding: (i) law of property and obligations, (ii) family law, and (iii) law of succession.[82] According to this research, Chomatenos significantly differs from other ecclesiastical judges because he is the only one who makes a very broad use of many civil law collections, treatises, and commentaries including the *Basilica*, the *Epitome* of *Novels* by Theodorus of Hermopolis, various *Novels* (e.g. of Romanos Lekapenos, Leo VI, Alexius I), the treatise on *peculia*, and the *Peira*. Moreover, as Papagianni notes, Chomatenos' main concern was to achieve a result that he himself considered just. This means that in some cases, he did not follow the letter of the law but followed practices that had been accepted and were in use among the population. From the decisions of the patriarchal court of Constantinople, a special reference is made to the decisions during the patriarchate of Matthew I (1397–1410), who was responsible for sixty

---

[79] *Odyssey*, 15.20-23. See in detail Penna, 'Classical Literature in Byzantine Legal Sources'.
[80] See in detail Penna, 'Classical Literature in Byzantine Legal Sources'.
[81] See Gastgeber, Mitsiou, Preiser-Kapeller, and Zervan, *A Companion to the Patriarchate of Constantinople* and Gastgeber, Mitsiou and Preiser-Kapeller, *The Register of the Patriarachate of Constantinople. An Essential Source for the History and Church of Late Byzantium*. For fourteenth century legal practice, see also Bénou, *Pour une nouvelle histoire du droit Byzantin. Théorie et pratique juridiques au XIVe siècle*.
[82] Papagianni, *Η νομολογία των εκκλησιαστικών δικαστηρίων της βυζαντινής και μεταβυζαντινής περιόδου σε θέματα περιουσιακού δικαίου*, 3 vols. The final outcomes of this research are summed up in the third volume (2010), 277–290. On Chomatenos, see also Simon, 'Byzantinische Provinzialjustiz'.

of the approximately 100 preserved rulings of the patriarchal court. The jurisprudence of the patriarchal court of Constantinople under Matthew I aims in general at the protection of the weak, or as Papagianni notes: 'Study of the relevant verdicts reveals the patriarch's struggle to serve the justice of God and protect the weak of society – at a time when all the inhabitants of Constantinople felt vulnerable.'[83]

Perhaps the most interesting observation when it comes to the jurisprudence of ecclesiastical courts, especially if we compare it with that of the secular courts, is that the Church has on more occasions shown flexibility and has adopted a more pragmatic approach to the social needs of the day.[84] A very characteristic example here is divorce by mutual consent. This method of dissolving a marriage continued to be practiced despite the legislative attempts to abolish or limit it. Based on the preserved judicial sources, the Church proved to be more daring than the State in resolving a marriage and more flexible and eager to adjust to the necessities of the litigant parties.[85] For example, based on the preserved ecclesiastical court decisions (e.g. Apokaukos, Patriarchate of Constantinople), the Church – which became responsible for dispute resolution arising from marriage after the eleventh century – became rather lenient when it came to divorce.[86]

1.7 When Does Byzantine Law End, or Does Byzantine Law End?

Up to now we have seen how Roman law 'became' Byzantine law, how Roman law evolved in the Eastern Roman Empire, and how significant the role of the *antecessors* was in that development. If the sixth century is crucial for the 'birth' of Byzantine law, the question is when does Byzantine law end? One can argue that Byzantine law ends in 1453 when the Ottomans conquered Constantinople, and the Roman Empire collapsed. Indeed, the year 1453 traditionally marks the end of the Eastern Roman Empire, the end of Byzantium, but this does not mean that everything that was Byzantine just stopped to exist. Even after the sack of Constantinople in 1453, one can see Byzantine influences in many fields including art, literature and – in our case – law. The Romanian historian Nicolae Iorga (1871–1940) wrote in 1935 an influential study entitled 'Byzance après

---

[83] Papagianni, 'Courts and justice'.
[84] Papagianni, *Η νομολογία των εκκλησιαστικών δικαστηρίων της βυζαντινής και μεταβυζαντινής περιόδου σε θέματα περιουσιακού δικαίου*, vol 3: 290.
[85] Examined in detail by Papagianni, 'Το διαζύγιο στο Βυζάντιο: Κοινωνικές αντιλήψεις, νομοθετική πολιτική και εκκλησιαστική πρακτική'.
[86] Papagianni, Ibid, especially 1371–1374.

Byzance', which examines the legacy of Byzantine civilization in Europe.[87] Iorga states: 'Byzantium is a synthesis of very different elements which come from everywhere, and which always remain open until the Byzantine idea in the end itself disappears'.[88]

Byzantine law continued to live and develop in Southeastern Europe even after the rise of the Ottomans. During the period of Ottoman rule (the so-called *Turkokratia*), justice was administered by an Ottoman official, the *kadi*, but local authorities were also allowed to judge cases involving non-Muslims.[89] Sultans issued official charters (*berats*) delegating judicial power to the patriarch and the metropolitans for the Orthodox Christians.[90] Thus ecclesiastical courts administered justice for the Christian population during the period of Ottoman rule. One should consider that the episcopal courts already had experience in judging cases, since optional episcopal jurisdiction had been allowed by the Byzantine emperors and had gradually expanded in both civil and criminal cases. Ecclesiastical courts, next to canon law, also applied the law included in the *Hexabiblos* of Harmenopoulos, a collection of laws made in the middle of the fourteenth century by a judge in Thessalonica named Constantinos Harmenopoulos.[91] Local customs also played a significant role, and in fact, in some cases, they were so important that the Greek authorities decided to write them down.[92] In 1835 under the rule of King Otto in Greece, it was ordered that the civil laws of the Byzantine emperors, as included in the *Hexabiblos*, would be valid until the promulgation of a civil code, which was then commissioned in Greece.[93] In that way, Byzantine-Roman law became official law in the new established Kingdom of Greece. The *Hexabiblos* was valid until 1946 when a Greek civil code was finally promulgated. Some provisions of Byzantine law are

---

[87] Iorga, '*Byzance après Byzance. Continuation de 'l'histoire de la vie Byzantine*'.
[88] This quotation from Maner, '"Byzance après Byzance" – Nicolae Iorga's Concept and its Aftermath', 31.
[89] See, for example, Kermeli, 'The Right to Choice: Ottoman Justice vis-á-vis Ecclesiastical and Communal Justice in the Balkans, Seventeenth-Nineteenth Centuries' and Kotzageorgis, 'Δικαιϊκός πλουραλισμός (legal pluralism) στην οθωμανική αυτοκρατορία: Οι χριστιανοί στα οθωμανικά και εκκλησιαστικά δικαστήρια πριν το Τανζιμάτ'.
[90] See Kermeli, cited above, especially p. 169 with references to studies of P. Konortas and E. Zachariadou. See also, Kotzageorgis, cited above, 10.
[91] On the *Hexabiblos*, see Pitsakis, *Κωνσταντίνου Ἁρμενοπούλου, Πρόχειρον Νόμων ἢ Ἑξάβιβλος*, in the introduction p. ζ´ – ρια´ and especially p. πθ´– ρια´, where the author examines the role of the *Hexabiblos* during the period of Ottoman rule and in the Greek State.
[92] About customs in Byzantium, see Bénou, *Pour une nouvelle histoire du droit Byzantin. Théorie et pratique juridiques au XIVᵉ siècle*, 109–124.
[93] Decree of 23 February/7th March 1835.

still applied nowadays in Greece for cases that deal with some legal rights that are established before 1946, that is, before the Greek civil code was adopted. For example, cases regarding ownership of immovable property, which is acquired by acquisitive prescription before 1946.[94] A case that had been in the spotlight for many years (2010–2019) in Greece concerned a dispute between the state and the Vatopedi monastery of the monastic community of Mount Athos regarding the ownership of Lake Vistonida and surrounding land. In trying to prove the ownership of these plots, the representatives of the Vatopedi monastery presented *inter alia* golden bulls (chrysobulls) issued by Byzantine emperors from the fourteenth century. The Greek judges – including Supreme Court judges – had thus to consider and interpret provisions of these Byzantine documents which concerned the disputed land titles.

2 How Is Byzantine Law Related to European Law, or Rethinking Byzantine Law

2.1 What Have the Romans Ever Done for Us?

It is true that our society is very different from that of the Romans. For example, Romans used slaves, and the concept of family was very different in Roman times than it is now. However, the basic legal questions remained the same throughout the centuries. For instance, how do you become the owner of a good? How do you lose ownership? What is the influence of good faith in legal transactions? Is there a remedy for the buyer who has bought a good that proves to have a defect? If someone has caused damage to someone else's property, are they liable under all circumstances? Roman jurists had discussed these kinds of questions in detail. To put it simply, they had discussed basic legal questions, and they had argued in for or against different solutions to legal problems and of relevant legal constructions. This explains why the writings of Roman jurists, even if they are old texts, are still nevertheless inspiring and useful for modern jurists, as well. We still can learn from their texts. We still can train our legal minds by studying their writings. For those interested in law, there is

---

[94] See, for example, the judgment of the Piraeus Court of Appeal no 557 in year 2024 (www.efeteio-peir.gr/?p=13239), which refers *inter alia* to fragments of the *Codex* and the *Digest* and the judgment of the Greek Supreme Court (Areios Pagos) no 2105 in 2022.
    (https://www.areiospagos.gr/nomologia/apofaseis_DISPLAY.asp?cd=HWDRG9RD L68KB8IK2ZKPV4WV7ZX12G&apof=2105_2022&info). For an overview of references to Roman-Byzantine law in modern Greek jurisprudence, see Dimopoulou, 'Το ρωμαϊκό και βυζαντινορωμαϊκό δίκαιο στη νομολογία των τελευταίων χρόνων'.

no expiration date for the writings of the Romans jurists. They have been serving as an inexhaustible source of inspiration for jurists for a very long time. As Peter Stein, a scholar par excellence who has studied Roman law in European culture, has phrased it, Roman law texts 'have constituted a kind of legal supermarket, in which lawyers of different periods have found what they needed at the time'.[95]

In fact, modern civil codes are to a significant part based on Roman law. Civil law or private law is the law that regulates conflicts between citizens; for example, disputes about a contract of sale or disputes about the acquisition of property. If one studies the modern civil codes in Greece, the Netherlands, France, Germany, Italy, Belgium, and in many more countries, one would realize that the core of these civil codes has been influenced by Roman law, especially in the field of law of obligations and property law.[96] Even before the promulgation of the first codifications (e.g. the Prussian civil code in 1794, the French civil code in 1804, the civil code of Austria in 1811, and the German civil code in 1900), Roman law had played for a very long time a significant role in Europe. From the time of the Middle Ages, Roman law was the basis of the so-called '*ius commune*', a common system of legal thought that was used in Western Europe from roughly the end of the eleventh century up to the first modern codifications of law at the end of the eighteenth century. But how did Roman law become the '*ius commune*' of Europe? We speak about the 'rediscovery' of Roman law in eleventh- and twelfth-century Western Europe, which began in Italy, in Bologna. But what was the Roman law that was rediscovered then? How was this Roman law transmitted, preserved, explained, and handed over to the West in the Middle Ages? In answering those questions, we will see that the Byzantines had a significant role to play.

2.2 It Is the Language, Stupid, or the 'Birth' of European Private Law

In the first part of this Element, we discussed Justinian's aim to restore the Roman Empire and the impressive legislative work that was achieved during his reign. We also saw how the Latin legislation of Justinian was translated and adopted in Greek by the sixth-century jurists and how gradually Roman law was 'transformed' into 'Byzantine' law in the Eastern Roman

---

[95] Stein, *Roman Law in European History*, 2.
[96] For the Roman law influence on the modern law of obligations, see for example, the monumental work by Zimmermann, *The law of Obligations. Roman Foundations of Civilian Tradition.*

empire. This was the fate of Justinian's legislation in the East. In other words, this was the evolution of law in the East. But what happened to the legislation of Justinian in the West?

In short, after the reign of Justinian from roughly the end of the sixth century up to the end of the eleventh century in the West, Roman law was somewhat forgotten. What do we mean by this? In the West, there were legal collections with some Roman elements and influences issued by Germanic rulers; for instance, the *Lex Romana Visigothorum*, also known as the Breviary of King Alaric II in 506 or the *Lex Romana Burgundionum* compiled by King Gundobad (474–516). Some scholars use the term 'Roman vulgar law' to characterize the law in the West from roughly the sixth century up to the eleventh century, which was a simplified and not so complicated Roman law.[97] The simplified Latin spoken in the early middle ages is called 'vulgar Latin': hence the name 'Roman vulgar law' does not mean that it was lewd or uncouth. So, there were undoubtedly some collections in the West with Roman law elements, but the fact is that the *Digest* was forgotten in the West between the end of the sixth century and the end of the eleventh century. As far as Roman jurisprudence is concerned, the *Digest* was the most important part of Justinian's legislation, because it consisted of fragments of the writings of the great Roman jurists. For people interested in legal thinking, this sophisticated text encapsulating Roman legal science, is a treasure. And it was this text, the *Digest*, that remained in the shadow in the West for many centuries.

All this changed at the end of the eleventh and beginning of the twelfth century. It is within that very period that the *Digest* was rediscovered in Bologna. Hence Roman law began to be studied in Italy and rather quickly, the study and application of Roman law was spread throughout Europe. When we speak of the 'rediscovery of Roman law' in the Middle Ages we mainly mean the rediscovery of the *Digest* in the roughly late eleventh century.[98] Today we possess only one sixth-century manuscript of the *Digest*, the so-called *Littera Florentina*, preserved at the library of Florence. There is not much information about the first professors who taught Roman law in Bologna. According to most scholars, it was presumably Irnerius (d. c. 1130), a teacher of liberal arts in Bologna one of the first who taught Roman law in Bologna.[99] Irnerius and other scholars

---

[97] See, Liebs, 'Roman Vulgar Law in Late Antiquity'. Liebs points out in this study that the term 'Roman vulgar law' should be used with caution.

[98] See, for example, Berman, *Law and Revolution: The Formation of the Western Legal Tradition*; Stein, *Roman Law in European History*.

[99] Hallebeek, 'Structure of Medieval Roman Law', 289.

of this period and the following centuries started writing comments in the margins of the manuscripts of Justinian's legislation. These comments and annotations were called *glossae*. Taking their name from the way they expanded the texts, by writing these *glossae* (= annotations) in the margins, Irnerius and his colleagues are also known as the 'glossators'. We do not know why this 'rediscovery of Roman law' occurred within this period, that is, around the end of the eleventh century and at that place, that is, Italy. A modern scholar has spoken of 'the Big Bang of Roman law' in the Middle Ages.[100] There are various theories about causes, but the key point is that there was a need for a law that could solve difficult legal problems in this time and place, not least because of the rise of commerce of the Italian cities. The *Digest* was a legal text in which you could find solutions to complicated legal dilemmas. In short, the time was ripe for the *Digest*.

Language was crucial in the 'rediscovery of Roman law' that took place in the Middle Ages in the West. As already mentioned, the emperor Justinian issued most of his legislation in Latin, which at the time was a problem for most of his subjects in the Eastern Roman Empire, since they were Greek-speaking and could not understand Justinian's legislation. However, the publication of Justinianic legislation in Latin was extremely fortuitous for later Western European legal history. In the eleventh- and twelfth-century Europe, Latin was a bit like English is today in that it was the most widely used common language. Since most of the legislation of Justinian was written in Latin, it was possible for the people of the Middle Ages to read it, understand it and use it in the West. In other words, if Justinian had issued his legislation in Greek, nobody in the Middle Ages would have cared about it and we would have had another story to tell for European private law. There was a saying in the Middle Ages: '*Graeca non leguntur*', which means 'Greek is not read'. It seems most copyists in the West simply dismissed Greek manuscripts since they could not understand them. It was thus fortunate for the West (and for the fate of Roman law) that the Eastern Roman emperor Justinian had issued most of his legislation in Latin.

2.3 What Have the Byzantines Ever Done for Us?

The Roman law that was rediscovered in medieval Italy was the Roman law that was codified by the Byzantine emperor Justinian. This Roman law later became part of the *ius commune* in Europe, part of the common legal thought

---

[100] Pennington, 'The "Big Bang": Roman Law in the Early Twelfth Century'.

in Europe and influenced later even modern codifications in Europe. Hence, to return to the question 'what have the Romans ever given us?' the answer is 'Roman law', indeed. But how? Through the Byzantines, via Justinian that is. This explains why Justinian has been characterized by some modern scholars as 'the legislator of Europe'. If you open any book on the history of law in Europe, you will find a section dedicated to the legislation of Justinian, the so-called *Corpus Iuris Civilis*. What you presumably will not find in these books is the fact that Justinian was an emperor of the Eastern Roman Empire or/and to what happened to Roman law in the East. Of course, there are a few exceptions, and I certainly exclude Greek publications on the history of law in Europe. My criticism applies mainly to English-language publications, which are the ones that are being broadly read.

In summary, let me emphasize that Roman law was somewhat forgotten in the West from the sixth up to the eleventh centuries AD; however, in the East, that is not the case. In the East, there is continuity of Roman law throughout the whole period of the Byzantine empire and even beyond that. I can understand that most European legal scholars are interested in the fate of Roman law in the West. However, since most of their publications ostensibly cover the history of law *in Europe*, they quite unfairly ignore the history of Roman law in a large part of Europe (i.e. in Southeastern Europe), where the Roman Empire existed for more than a thousand years. Moreover, this omission is especially unfair because, as I have explained, it is in that part of Europe that Roman law was *always* present. I believe that by dismissing the fate of Roman law in the East you are only telling your audience half of the story. In other words, it is understandable that modern scholars in their publications are interested in the development of Roman law in the West; after all, that is their focus. I do not expect detailed explorations of law in the East in their publications, but at least some reference to the law in the Eastern Roman Empire could signal or hint to the audience that there is more to story of Roman law in Europe.

Several authoritative books present misunderstandings about Byzantine law or reveal ignorance about the importance of Roman law in the East and the value of Roman-Byzantine law for the European legal tradition. Some scholars write, for example, that Justinian's legislation or the *Corpus Iuris Civilis* fell out of use in the eastern Roman Empire.[101] That is not correct. Justinianic law or the *Corpus Iuris Civilis* or Roman law was always present in the East. It is true that it was adapted into Greek, and

---

[101] Gordley, *The Jurists*, 2. Let me clarify that this is an excellent book which I have used for many years in my classes as well.

it evolved, but Roman law was never forgotten in the Eastern Roman Empire. Justinian's codification remained always the bedrock of Byzantine law. To phrase it differently, the *Corpus Iuris Civilis* did fall out of use in the West and not in the East, but I wonder how many modern scholars know this other, half story of the *Corpus Iuris Civilis* in the East, in Byzantium that is.

I will only mention one Byzantine work here that reflects the deep significance of the *Corpus Iuris Civilis* in Eastern Roman Empire. We have already seen that the language of Justinian's legislation was a problem for most of his subjects. The *antecessors*, the law professors at the time of Justinian started translating Justinian's legislation in Greek which led to the 'birth' of Byzantine law. Gradually in due time, there were several Greek versions or summaries of the parts of Justinian's legislation, for example, of the *Digest* or of the *Code*. This created confusion about which versions were valid as applicable law. That is why at the end of the ninth century, the Byzantine emperors decided to proceed upon into the so-called 'purge/cleansing of the ancient laws' (ἀνακάθαρσις τῶν παλαιῶν νόμων), a clarification of the laws, that is, of the many Greek versions that existed of Justinian's legislation. The result was the *Basilica*, a massive compilation of laws consisting of sixty books that rendered the different parts of Justinian's legislation in Greek. The term *Basilica* ('τὰ Βασιλικὰ νόμιμα') means literally 'the imperial laws'.

Thus, the *Basilica* is a massive legal collection issued around 900, containing Justinianic law, but in Greek. Instead of having many different Greek versions and summaries of the *Digest*, the *Code*, and so on, the compilers made one large text, which consisted of all parts of Justinian's legislation, that is, a Greek-language *Corpus Iuris Civilis*.[102] The *Basilica*-compilers did not translate at that point the different parts of Justinian's legislation. Instead, they used Greek versions that already existed of the *Digest*, of the *Code*, and so on, most of which had been created by Byzantine jurists of the sixth century, namely the *antecessors*.[103] For example, they mainly used a Greek translation of the *antecessor* Thalelaeus for the text of the *Code*. In other words, the compilers of the *Basilica* did what any person would have done out of a natural inclination that we all have as human beings: namely, laziness. Why translate the parts of Justinian's legislation into Greek if you already have such Greek translations or

---

[102] Little of Justinian's *Institutes* is included in the *Basilica*. The *Novels* were in their majority published in Greek anyway.
[103] See in detail Penna and Meijering, *A Sourcebook on Byzantine Law*, 123–129.

summaries of these parts at your disposal? The *Basilica* simply reorganized and collated the existing translations to compile the complete *Corpus Iuris Civilis* in Greek. In some cases, the *Basilica* compilers used a Greek equivalent word for a Latin technical term. In other words, they sometimes attempted to 'exhellenizein' (ἐξελληνίζειν), that is, to use Greek words for the Latin legal terms. We know these Greek adaptations, the *exhellenismoi*, were not all made at the same time because they are not always the same in the surviving manuscripts.

From the tenth century onwards comments, that is scholia, were added to the text of the *Basilica*. These scholia were comments from the *antecessors* which were added to the *Basilica* text because they helped explain it. Just as the *antecessors*' students needed some commentary to understand Justinianic law in the sixth century, so too their medieval counterparts wanted that commentary alongside their Greek-language version of Justinianic law. These scholia are known as the 'old' *Basilica* scholia because they date from the sixth century. But there is also a second group of comments which were written by Byzantine jurists in the eleventh and twelfth centuries and were added in the *Basilica* text and are known as the 'new' *Basilica* scholia. These later scholia are directly linked to the revival of legal studies that took place in Constantinople in the middle of the eleventh century. Around 1054, a law school was founded in Constantinople. It is worth noting that this revival of legal studies in the Byzantine capital took place in roughly the same period in which the 'rediscovery' of Roman law took place in the West in Bologna. The conditions however in which both revivals of law took place were very different. The law school in Constantinople can be considered more as a favour to one person, Ioannes Xiphilinos, an intellectual of that time who was appointed by the emperor as head of the law school in Constantinople. Xiphilinos became the so-called '*nomophylax*' (νομοφύλαξ), that is, the 'guardian of the laws'. Xiphilinos and other jurists of the eleventh and twelfth centuries wrote also scholia around the text of the *Basilica* and these scholia are known as the 'new' *Basilica* scholia to distinguish them from the 'old' *Basilica* scholia.

One must be cautious when dealing with the 'new' *Basilica* scholia. Although traditionally there is a distinction between 'old' and 'new' *Basilica* scholia, sometimes it is not easy to draw a clear line and make this distinction. The reason for this is that several of the 'new' scholia incorporate older material, or because *Basilica* scholia can consist of different layers. To understand this observation, one must consider the manuscripts. If there is an 'old' scholion written in the margin, and a later jurist adds something new to that note, is it an 'old' or a 'new' scholion? This is a ubiquitous problem when dealing with any scholia, that is especially pronounced in Byzantine legal sources. As is said in Byzantine law, 'things are not always what they seem'.[104] This is not the place to get into the whole discussion of the distinction between 'old' and 'new' *Basilica* scholia.[105] It is sufficient to say that, in some cases, the 'new' *Basilica* scholia can tell us something about the Byzantine legal thought and practice of the eleventh and twelfth centuries. This is especially interesting because this period is the same period in which Roman law was rediscovered in the West. This is the period in which the glossators began to write their scholia (*glossae*) in the margins of the manuscripts of Roman law in Bologna.

And whereas the *glossae*, that is, the annotations made by Western legal scholars have been studied in detail by modern scholars, very few scholars occupy themselves with the Byzantine '*glossae*', that is, the 'new' *Basilica* scholia, which are comments also on the *Corpus Iuris Civilis* but in Greek written by Byzantine jurists of the eleventh and twelfth centuries. To speak the sad truth, most of the modern scholars of legal history do not even know that Byzantine jurists also wrote scholia on the *Corpus Iuris Civilis*. If we investigate the Byzantine legal tradition, we can conclude that the Byzantine jurists are closer to the Roman texts since Roman law was never interrupted in Byzantium. A good example are the 'old' *Basilica* scholia, which I have already referred to. They derive from the teaching of the *antecessors*, the law professors at the time of Justinian. As I have already mentioned in the first part, some of these *antecessors* were members of the committees that drafted the *Digest*, the *Code*, the *Institutes*, that is, the parts of Justinian's legislation. For example, the *antecessor* Dorotheus was a member of the committees that had drafted the *Digest*, the *Code* (second version), and the *Institutes*; the *antecessor* Theophilus had been a member of the committees that drafted the *Code* (first version) and the *Institutes*. These *antecessors* knew very well the material, namely Roman law even before it was codified by Justinian. Their scholia can therefore help us understand even classical Roman law up to some extent. This is something that has been stressed among others by Frits Brandsma and has been highlighted by other scholars as well.[106]

---

[104] See also the observations of Ludwig Burgmann and Marie Theres Fögen in Burgmann and Fögen, 'Florilegium Lesbiacum', here especially 126–127.

[105] For this distinction and for examples of both kind of scholia with English translations, see Penna and Meijering, *A Sourcebook on Byzantine Law*, 137–143 and 152–164.

[106] Brandsma, 'The Usefulness of the Byzantine Tradition to the Interpretation of the *Corpus Iuris Civilis*' and other publications by Hylkje de Jong and myself, for example.

2.4 Comparing the Western to the Eastern Legal Tradition

When examining Roman law in the Middle Ages in a classic monograph, Paul Vinogradoff spoke of 'a ghost story'.[107] Other scholars have spoken of the many lives of Roman law. If that is the case with Roman law, then Byzantine law (i.e. the Roman law as it was developed in the Eastern Roman Empire) is not even a ghost story. Byzantine law does not even have one life – at least for most modern scholars. In fact, the bitter truth is that Byzantine law is essentially bypassed in modern books that refer to the history of law in Europe, apart from Greek publications. References to Byzantine law are from non-existent to rare in modern foreign language books on European history of law. Just as Byzantine history was neglected for a long period from the History of Europe, the same goes for Byzantine law. I argue that it makes sense to include Byzantine law in modern publications of History of European law not just because it was after all a Byzantine emperor (Justinian) who gave us Roman law but also because in Byzantium, in the Eastern Roman empire, as I explained, there was always a continuation of Roman law. Furthermore, I think there is a need to examine the Western and Eastern legal traditions *comparatively*. To put it simply, all historians agree that Justinian's *Corpus Iuris Civilis* is the basis of modern laws. It makes therefore sense to see how this *Corpus Iuris Civilis* was developed in the West, how it was developed in the East and to make the necessary comparisons.

By studying the Western and Eastern legal traditions comparatively, we will be perhaps able to get rid of some misunderstandings concerning Byzantine law or Byzantine history in general. To give just one example, during the 55th Spring Symposium of Byzantine Studies in 2024 in Kent, which was dedicated to Byzantine justice, I made a comparison of the writings of two authors.[108] The first was Cesare Beccaria (1738–1794) who was an Italian jurist and one of the great names of the Enlightenment. The second author was Leo VI the Wise (866–912), the Byzantine emperor who produced different kinds of writings including a great number of laws, *Novels*. Beccaria is traditionally considered the father of modern criminal law. In 1764, he wrote the treatise 'On Crimes and Punishments' which laid down fundamental principles of criminal law. Beccaria was, according

---

[107] Vinogradoff, *Roman Law in Medieval Europe*, 4: 'The story I am about to tell is, in a sense, a ghost story. It treats of a second life of Roman Law after the demise of the body in which it first saw the light.'

[108] The extended version of this lecture will be published under the title 'Justice in Byzantium: blind or biased?' in the relevant volume that is now prepared and edited by the conveners of the 55th Spring Symposium, Alwis and Franco (eds.).

to the prevailing opinion, the first who spoke about fair punishment emphasizing the proportionality between crime and punishment and the ineffectiveness of excessively harsh punishments. However, was that the case? Was Beccaria the first to do that? If one reads the laws of Leo VI the Wise, one would be surprised to see that Leo had also addressed the same issues with Beccaria in criminal law. Leo had mentioned, for example, in one of his laws that: 'Fair punishment exists when the guilty is subjected to a punishment proportionate to the gravity of the offense, for if the price for his expiation is greater than [his] fault, then, in my opinion, the sense of justice is not satisfied.'[109] I think that modern jurists would be rather surprised to find out that these lines derive from a Byzantine emperor from the late ninth century. Byzantium is, after all, still considered – at least by some – as a decadent, backward theocratic society.

Just as the writings of Beccaria can be compared to that of Leo VI the Wise as far as they both treat the same questions and issues of criminal law, so could the writings of Latin canonists be compared to Byzantine ones. I found very inspiring the comparison that Clarence Gallagher made between the Latin canonist Gratian and the Byzantine canonist Balsamon who both lived in the twelfth century.[110] Gratian is one of the most renown canonists in the West and author of the *Concordia discordantium canonum* (= Harmonization of Discordant Canons), better known as the *Decretum*, which became the most important collection of canon law and was used as a textbook in Bologna.[111] Balsamon is one of the best-known Byzantine canonists, mainly because of his commentary on the *Nomocanon in Fourteen Titles*. Gallagher compared the method and approach of these two canonists and discussed some examples of their work. He was the first who treated these two canonists together and published a study in comparative canonistic methodology.

It is indeed striking that there are practically no comparative studies of the Byzantine and the Western tradition also in the field of Canon law. Such potential comparisons can also help us understand better the evolution of some basic principles in modern law. To mention but one example, the rule of the *pacta sunt servanda* meaning 'agreements must

---

[109] 'Τὸ μὲν γὰρ κατὰ τρόπον τοῦ ἁμαρτήματος τὸν ἐξημαρτηκότα κολάζεσθαι τοῦτο δικαίου ἐκδίκησις, τὸ δὲ μείζω τοῦ πταίσματος ἀπαιτεῖσθαι τὴν εἴσπραξιν οὐκ οἶμαι σῴζειν τὴν ὑπὲρ τοῦ δικαίου προαίρεσιν', from *Novel* 62 of Leo VI the Wise in Troianos, *Οι Νεαρές του Λέοντος ς' του Σοφού*, 206, lines 8–11; For the relevant fragment and the comparison made to Beccaria, see in detail Penna, 'Justice in Byzantium: blind or biased?'

[110] Gallagher, 'Gratian and Theodore Balsamon: Two Twelfth-Century Canonistic Methods Compared'.

[111] In Bologna, both Roman and Canon law were taught.

be kept' implies that, when two parties willingly and knowingly enter into a contract, the terms of that contract should be upheld by both parties; it is binding. Parties are free to determine the content of their contracts themselves. In civil law, we call this freedom of contracts, which is a fundamental principle in modern civil law. As already mentioned, the core of modern European civil law – mainly property law and the law of obligations – is based on Roman law. Yet, the principle of *pacta sunt servanda*, which forms the cornerstone of modern contract law, does not derive from Roman law. It is well known that canon law played a significant role in the West for the evolution of this principle. This is something that has been notably studied in the West including the writings of Latin canonists. Yet, this principle was also adopted and developed in Byzantium, something that perhaps is not well known. It is worth comparing here the evolution of this basic legal principle in Western and Byzantine sources, especially because in both legal traditions religious influences did play a role in the development of this principle.[112]

Moreover, by studying the Western and Eastern legal traditions comparatively, one can see whether there is a stronger common legal heritage between the West and the East than it is commonly thought. Several times, I have seen in my research an interaction and mutual influence between the Western and Eastern legal traditions, perhaps more than one would expect.[113] Byzantium was, after all, never cut off from other nations and cultures. Especially in the period of the eleventh and twelfth centuries – which is the period of the 'rediscovery' of Roman law – and with the growth of Italian cities, there are connections and interactions between Byzantium and the West in various areas. Let us not forget that the Italians had established their own districts in the Byzantine capital within this period. Byzantine emperors had granted immovable property in Constantinople to the Italians from the tenth century onwards. These possessions stemmed from the need of the merchants for places in which they could safely store their merchandise. However, gradually these areas were extended. Italians had their own districts in the Byzantine capital and in fact they occupied important commercial areas.[114] As foreigners settled in Byzantine cities and established their businesses there, it was inevitable that foreign practices, customs, and laws became known to the Byzantines

---

[112] For a first approach, see Penna, 'Religious influences on medieval civil law. The *pacta sunt servanda* principle in Byzantine and medieval Western law'.
[113] See Section 2.5.
[114] See Magdalino, 'The Maritime Neighborhoods of Constantinople: Commercial and Residential Functions, Sixth to Twelfth Centuries'.

and vice versa. The movement of people within the empire brought inevitably the movement of cultural and legal practices. In the following section, I will give some examples of the interaction between the Western and Eastern legal traditions and the benefit of comparing the two traditions for a better understanding of the European legal heritage.

2.5 Unravelling the Common Legal Past of Europe[115]

Nowadays, a key element in the European structure is without doubt the common legal mechanism that is being formed; the European legislator must face a challenge in formatting laws which will apply to so many countries and so many different legal systems. But was there a common legal route behind today's Europe? What is the information we obtain from acts of that time regarding the legal relations between the Western and Eastern parts of Europe? And, can Byzantine law play a role in unravelling the common European legal past? My first book investigated these questions regarding the Mediterranean part of Europe in the Middle Ages focussing on Byzantine material.[116]

For that research, I studied and analysed all Byzantine imperial documents referring to Venice, Pisa, and Genoa in chronological order up to 1204 from a legal viewpoint. The aim was to examine the legal issues that arose from these documents in detail; for example, grants of immovable property to the Italians, issues of jurisdiction and competent courts for the Italians, maritime and salvage law provisions (e.g. what happened to the goods for example of Italians in case of a shipwreck and salvage provisions). These documents consisted mainly of privileges granted by the Byzantine Emperors in favour of the Italian cities, the so-called chrysobulls (i.e. imperial grants certified with gold seals), which were in reality treaties between Byzantines and Italians. The material also consisted of imperial letters in which information was given about the negotiations which took place beforehand. These Byzantine documents formed excellent material for answering the research questions for the following reasons: they referred to practical legal issues and gave information not only on the actual regulation of legal issues but also on the 'making of' the legal solutions chosen. Moreover, they were promulgated within a period that

---

[115] Parts of this section are taken from Penna, 'Odd Topics, Old Methods and the Cradle of the Ius Commune: Byzantine Law and the Italian City-States'.
[116] Penna, *The Byzantine Imperial Acts to Venice, Pisa and Genoa, 10th–12th Centuries. A Comparative Legal Study*.

was crucial for the 'rediscovery' of Roman law in the West and, finally, they offered a link between the Eastern and the Western parts of Europe.

In the second part of that research, a comparative analysis of the common legal issues was made with other Byzantine and Western sources of that period. For example, comparisons were made with Byzantine imperial acts directed at monasteries of that time in order to investigate similarities and differences in the procedures followed and the terminology used. Regarding the Western sources, comparisons were mainly made with Crusader charters for the following reason. The eleventh and twelfth centuries were also the time of the Crusades and the newly established Crusader states had good contacts with Venice, Pisa, and Genoa. The three Italian cities were granted important privileges by the Crusader leaders. In that respect, the privilege charters of the Crusader leaders shared similarities with the privilege acts of the Byzantine Emperors. Legal issues that were regulated in the privilege charters of the Crusader leaders were also regulated in the Byzantine imperial privileges granted to the Italian cities, something that is not so strange since in many cases the legal questions were the same.[117] What happens, for example, when a Venetian dies within the Byzantine empire or the Crusader states and has left no testament? Who is to inherit his estate? Or, what happens when a shipwreck of Pisan ship takes place with the Byzantine empire or within the territory of the Crusader states? Who is owner of the goods that have been salvaged, for example?

There are enough legal examples in my material that prove the legal interaction between both the Byzantine and the Western world. The Italians accepted practices that corresponded to Byzantine legal practice, for example, in issues dealing with the granting of immovable property. From the examples referring to justice, we can also observe that the Italians encountered the Byzantine judicial system. The Byzantines in their turn accepted the jurisdiction of a foreign judge – even for mixed cases – within their capital and by doing so they must have become acquainted with the administration of justice by this foreign judge. In the legal provisions dealing with maritime law, there are more points of legal interaction between both sides. For example, the resolution of the maritime conflict in this period between the Byzantines and the Genoese by a measure that is strongly reminiscent of the practice of the *ius represaliarum* shows the Western influence on Byzantine legal practice. It illustrates how Byzantine

---

[117] For this, see Penna, 'Similar Problems, Similar Solutions? Byzantine Chrysobulls and Crusader Charters on Legal Issues Regarding the Italian Maritime Republics'.

practice appropriated a merchants' custom linked to Western Europe, a custom that later influenced the field of international law in medieval and early modern Europe, that is, reprisals.[118]

In short, evidence of legal interaction between both Byzantines and Italians indicates that there was a common legal understanding between Byzantium and the Italian cities, between East and West, in the eleventh and twelfth centuries. The study of these Byzantine documents gives us a picture of how both jurisdictions, Western and Eastern, influenced each other. This enables us to give a more detailed and complete picture of the early stages of the *ius commune*, which forms the beginning of European private law and subsequently an insight into how legal development can contribute to the common ties of modern Europe. My research placed a very small piece of the puzzle of how a common European legal heritage was formed. There is so much work to be done in that field and especially in comparing Byzantine material to its Western counterpart.

To conclude this section, the study, analysis, and comparison of documents of the medieval period at a European level help us to determine whether today's European countries were already bound by common legal forms, long before the modern age. Comparing Byzantine and Western documents from a legal viewpoint can help us better understand the birth and shaping of the *ius commune* and the medieval roots of private international law and subsequently the formation of our European legal identity. It is thus worth studying Byzantine law for this reason. In fact, the study of Byzantine law can in some cases even help us examine the interactions between Byzantine and Islamicate worlds. For example, the translation, adaptation and transmission of Byzantine legal texts into Arabic (i.e. the *Procheiros Nomos*, the *Ecloga*, etc.)[119] or comparing, for example, maritime practices in Byzantine and Islamic legal texts.[120]

2.6 From Harmenopoulos to Windscheid and Beyond

The comprehensive history of European law is not only helped by placing eastern and western legal texts in comparative dialog, but by putting Byzantine legal sources in a broader perspective. What do I mean by this?

---

[118] See in detail Penna, 'Piracy and reprisal in Byzantine waters: resolving a maritime conflict between Byzantines and Genoese at the end of the twelfth century'.

[119] See, for example, Pahlitzsch, *Der arabische Procheiros Nomos. Untersuchung und Edition der arabischen Übersetzung eines byzantinischen Rechtstextes*.

[120] See on this, the works by Hassan Salih Khalilieh and especially his book *Admiralty and Maritime Laws in the Mediterranean Sea (ca. 800–1050). The Kitāb Akriyat al-Sufun vis-à-vis the Nomos Rhodion Nautikos*.

For some of the Byzantine legal sources, it is worth not only looking into the actual text and studying that material as such, but it is worth looking into the 'journey' and transmission of this source in the West, if any. In this section, I will try to give an example of such an approach. I will refer to a Byzantine legal source which had a great influence in Southeastern Europe and show that this source has also a significant influence in the West, something that is not so known. On the basis of various testimonies, I will also propose a hypothesis about the influence that this Byzantine text had in the West, which may seem at first sight radical to some.

The source that I am referring to is the *Hexabiblos*, a legal manual dating from the middle of the fourteenth century and was compiled by a judge in Thessalonica named Constantine Harmenopoulos. Is it possible to link the Byzantine *Hexabiblos* to the German jurist Bernhard Windscheid (1817–1892) who played a significant role in the drafting up of the German civil code of 1900? In other words, how is the Byzantine fourteenth-century *Hexabiblos* connected to the German civil code of 1900? This is something that I will attempt to do in this section in an effort of showing the effectiveness of restudying Byzantine legal sources in a greater perspective.

First, a few words about the *Hexabiblos*. This legal collection is also known as the *Procheiron Nomōn Konstantinou tou Harmenopoulou* (Πρόχειρον Νόμων Κωνσταντίνου τοῦ Ἀρμενοπούλου = Handbook of Laws of Constantine Harmenopoulos) and in Latin '*Promptuarium iuris, Constantino Harmenopulo authore*'. Harmenopoulos' aim was to create a legal handbook that was easy to use in legal practice. This is implied in the Greek title 'procheiron nomōn' since the word 'procheiros' means something that is 'at hand', 'easy'; in this case, it is an 'easy handbook of laws'. As Constantine Pitsakis (1944–2012) observed, many people seem to forget the nature of this work: it was neither the result of a learned committee; nor ordered by an emperor; nor an official law.[121] The fact that many people forget both exactly what the *Hexabiblos* is and its influence in future centuries has created a rather unfair criticism of this collection. However, because of its simplicity, the *Hexabiblos* became an influential text in the Eastern part of Europe. It was rendered many times into Modern Greek, reprinted several times in Greece, and used in legal practice up to the promulgation of the first Greek civil code in 1946. The *Hexabiblos* was also translated into Slavic languages and was spread throughout the Balkan region. It also received much attention in Western Europe, as is proven by

---

[121] Pitsakis, Κωνσταντίνου Ἀρμενοπούλου, Πρόχειρον Νόμων ἢ Ἑξάβιβλος, in the Introduction, να'.

its multiple critical editions and translations. There are thirteen editions of the *Hexabiblos* in the West in Greek, Latin, and German.

Perhaps the most surprising testimony of the *Hexabiblos* in the intellectual life of the West is the one that Constantine Pitsakis has revealed: the reference to the *Hexabiblos* by the dramatist Jean Racine (1639–1699). Racine was one of the most known French dramatists of the seventeenth century. In 1668, he wrote the comedy *Les Plaideurs* (= The Litigants). The plot of this play is an adaptation of Aristophane's *Wasps*. The protagonist in Racine's comedy was a judge named Dandin, who was addicted to courtroom life and was obsessed with judging cases. His son, Léandre, in order to please his father's obsession, sets up a fake court at his house so his father can 'judge' some domestic cases at his ease. A 'case' is brought before the judge Dandin. The defendant is a dog, which is brought to trial because he ate an appetizing capon. His lawyer (L'Intimé), in his speech before the domestic court, supports his legal arguments by referring to the most famous names that he can think of in the field of law. He refers to Aristotle, to the known legal scholar humanist Jacques Cujas and to … Harmenopoulos. Here is the relevant fragment of the play:

L' INTIMÉ: […] Aristote, *primo, peri Politikon*, Dit fort bien…	LAWYER: […] Aristotle, *primo peri politikon* says very properly…
DANDIN: Avocat, il s'agit d'un chapon, Et non point d'Aristote et de sa *Politique*. […]	DANDIN: Lawyer, this is about a capon and not about **Aristotle** and his *Politics*. […]
DANDIN: Au fait.	DANDIN: To the point.
L' INTIMÉ: Rebuffe…	LAWYER: Rebuff…
DANDIN: Au fait, vous dis-je.	DANDIN: To the point, I say.
L' INTIMÉ: Le grand Jacques…	LAWYER: The great **Jacques**… (= Cujas)
DANDIN: Au fait, au fait, au fait.	DANDIN: To the point, to the point, to the point.
L' INTIMÉ: **Harmeno Pul**, *in Prompt*…	LAWYER: **Harmeno Pul** (= Harmenopoulos) in his *Prompt*… (= *Promptuarium iuris*)
DANDIN: Ho! je te vais juger.	DANDIN: Oh! I will sentence you.
L' INTIMÉ: Ho! vous êtes si prompt![122]	LAWYER: Oh! You are so hasty!

I would like to add here two remarks about this play by Racine. First, that even though the play was not a raging success from its premier, it gradually became very popular in the circles of French aristocracy. It was

---

[122] Racine, *Les Plaideurs* (this fragment is from the third scene of the third act), cited from: https://fr.wikisource.org/wiki/Les_Plaideurs/Barbin,_1669.

even played at Versailles before the court of Louis XIV of France. Imagine – there, at the pinnacle of the Sun King's intellectual scene, the name of Harmenopoulos being mentioned next to that of Aristotle and to the eminent legal humanist Jacques Cujas (1522–1590), the 'great Jacques'... This is rather a unique honour for an author deriving from the Byzantine legal tradition, which was mostly looked upon (and still is?) as a decadent legal tradition. A second observation here is that Racine did not have legal education. The speech of the lawyer in his play must have been based on the average legal speeches of that time. The legal sources that he refers to must have been the commonly known legal sources used by a normal sensible lawyer. It is also remarkable that Racine does not refer to many names in the legal field but only a few, characteristic ones and Harmenopoulos is one of these! How would Racine have known of Harmenopoulos? Could this be an indication that the *Hexabiblos* of Harmenopoulos was used at that time even in French courtrooms? In any case, the reference of Harmenopoulos by Racine is quite remarkable and has attracted the attention of only two or three scholars up to now.

There are other interesting testimonies concerning the use of the *Hexabiblos* in Germany. The *Hexabiblos* had been translated into German by Justinus Göbler (or Gobler, 1504–1567) and was published in Frankfurt in 1564 (and republished in 1566 and 1576). Göbler describes in the preface to his translation that he has made this German translation because of the 'common benefit' (*gemeinem nuz*) and for those interested in the text from the jurists, the judges, officers, writers, and others whose Latin was not so good to help them. There is another valuable testimony to the German translation of the *Hexabiblos*. In 1832, the Bavarian prince Otto was appointed King of Greece by the three Great Powers of that time (Britain, France, and Russia). Because Otto was a minor, a regency of three men was also appointed to govern until Otto reached adulthood. One of the regency members was Georg Ludwig von Maurer (1790–1872). Von Maurer was responsible for justice, ecclesiastical, and education issues of the New Greek State. Von Maurer published a book referring to the Greek public, ecclesiastical, and private affairs before the Greek War of Independence and up to the first years of the regency. In that book, he referred to customs and laws in Greece referencing particularly the *Hexabiblos*. Von Maurer wrote that he owned a copy of the German translation. He also made the comment that there were three editions of this work within twelve years in Germany, which meant – according to him – that it must have been useful for the law students in Germany. Presumably it must have been used in German courts too, judging from the preface and the cover of the German translation of the *Hexabiblos*, where it is mentioned that it is made for judges, officers, jurists, and courtroom practitioners. Hence, it seems that the *Hexabiblos* was used in German legal practice.

At this point, I would like to propose a hypothesis which some might regard as a stretch. The actual structure and the order of treatment of the legal material by Harmenopoulos is remarkable. The Byzantine judge moves away from the threefold Roman division (i.e. persons, things, lawsuits), and he divides civil law into the following five parts: (i) general principles, (ii) property law, (iii) law of obligations, (iv) family law, and (v) law of succession. As far as I know, Harmenopoulos is the first who chose to have first a general part and then move on to specific subjects of civil law, a structure that we see nowadays in most of our modern civil codes. This division of material, which does not derive from Roman law, is something that we observe for the first time in the West much later, nearly five centuries after Harmenopoulos. It was used for the first time in the German civil code that was promulgated in 1900 (the BGB = *Bürgerliches Gesetzbuch*).

The German civil code was influenced by the doctrine of the Pandectists. The Pandectists was a nineteenth-century German legal movement, which derived from the so-called Historical school of jurisprudence and aimed in the scientific application of Roman law. They took their name from the *Pandects*, that is the *Digest* of Justinian, and they wanted a systematization of Roman law for contemporary use. Bernhard Windscheid (1817–1892), one of the best-known Pandectists, was one of the members of the committee that drafted the German civil code. Even though he left the commission before the work was complete, he nevertheless had a very considerable influence on the final draft. There is indeed a lot of Roman law influence on the German civil code; for example, the Roman contribution is dominant in the field of obligations. However, as mentioned earlier, the structure of the German civil code moves away from the traditional threefold structure of Roman law (persons, things, lawsuits). Characteristic in the structure of the German civil code is the rule moving from 'general to particular', something that Harmenopoulos also adopts in his *Hexabiblos*. In the German civil code, first there is a general part (book one) setting out rules common to all kinds of legal transactions and includes the part of law of persons dealing with legal capacity. Then follow four books devoted especially to obligations, things, family law, and succession law.

Scholars have pointed out that this division of the material in the German civil code (having first a general part and then moving to other subjects of civil law) is a direct influence of the so-called late natural law lawyers, known also as the *mos geometricus* movement which flourished in Germany in the late seventeenth and eighteenth centuries.[123] The scholars of this movement used a method of legal reasoning that treats law as a science, deducing legal rules from a small number of fundamental, self-evident principles, something that resembles rules of classical geometry. The Pandectists were influenced in their methods by the late natural law lawyers and were also interested, in classifications, definitions, schematic approaches. Yet, given that the *Hexabiblos* was known in German legal circles, I wonder whether our humble Byzantine Harmenopoulos perhaps played indirectly a role in this development of the structure of the material of civil law in Germany. At minimum, this is a possibility. Let me briefly explain my arguments in favour of this hypothesis.

First, we have seen that there was a German translation of the *Hexabiblos* already from the sixteenth century, a translation that was republished twice in Germany in a rather short period. This implies that there was a need to republish the text because people were using it. Second, we have also seen that there are a few testimonies of using the *Hexabiblos* in German legal practice (the preface of the German translation implies this and the testimony of Von Maurer mentioned earlier). This means that the text of the *Hexabiblos* was obviously circulating among German legal scholars from the sixteenth century onwards. Would it be so strange, then, to suggest that German legal scholars had noticed the radical, non-Roman structure of the *Hexabiblos* and perhaps had already adopted it in their studies because it was more practical? It is difficult to imagine that these jurists read the *Hexabiblos* but not think about it. Right now, what I propose is just a hypothesis but a better and more thorough investigation of German sources (jurisprudence, correspondence of legal circles, etc.) may well strengthen the idea that the structure of the *Hexabiblos* had some influence on the structure of the German civil code. We can be certain that the mere plausibility of this suggestion shows the potential usefulness of comparing the Western legal tradition to the Eastern one.

2.7 The Future of Byzantine Law

Nearly forty years ago, Alexander Kazhdan criticized the approach of legal historians to Byzantine law and posed the question whether a new history of Byzantine law was needed.[124] According to Kazhdan, historians of Byzantine

---

[123] Samuel Pufendorf (1632–1694), Christian Thomasius (1655–1728), and Christian Wolff (1679–1754) are three important representatives of this movement.

[124] His paper was first given in Frankfurt in 1981, and in 1989, it was published, see Kazhdan, 'Do We Need a New History of Byzantine Law?'

law focussed on the normative texts, that is, the formal sources of law and did not take into account other sources, for example, non-legal sources and documentary evidence. Bernard Stolte responded to Kazhdan's remarks and explained the obvious, that namely legal historians have, in principle, different aims and interests than historians have.[125] In the words of Stolte: 'Kazhdan's complaint is an example of the different expectations by lawyers and historians when the turn to legal history. Even when they agree on what "is the law", they often are interested in different aspects, and unfortunately these interests appear to be mutually exclusive.'[126] This does not mean the legal historians and historians cannot work together, or that it is possible that they might have the same interests and in that case, as Stolte phrases it 'they would be fools not to try to profit from each other's work'.[127]

Personally, I think that there is much more common ground for co-operation between historians and legal historians who occupy themselves with Byzantine law (the latter being a rare species). It is, for example, important that the historians who study and use Byzantine legal sources know what these sources exactly are. I say this because it is an issue that can be tricky in Byzantine legal sources. Their dating does not necessarily mean that they reflect the law of the period in which they have been issued. Take for example the *Basilica*. They were issued at the end of the ninth century, but they reflect mainly Justinianic law. Or take the *Basilica* scholia. You can avoid misunderstandings if you know that some of the *Basilica* scholia do not date from the sixth century but from the eleventh or twelfth century.[128] In the last twelve or so years, I had the opportunity to co-operate on many occasions with historians, I have learned a lot from them and I hope that I have helped somehow in the study of Byzantine legal sources. In most cases, the historians reached out to me, to my great benefit. Not only did I have the chance to study better some of the Byzantine legal sources, but the historians' questions and approaches pushed me to think of some legal subjects in a broader and sometimes more creative way than I would have otherwise. There is not really a right or wrong way of dealing with Byzantine law: it depends on what your interests are and on what you wish to find out.[129] But, whatever your goals, you need to know what you are studying, in this case what the legal source actually is.[130]

---

[125] Stolte, 'Not new but novel. Notes on the historiography of Byzantine law'.
[126] Ibid., 265.   [127] Ibid.
[128] See above the discussion about the 'old' and 'new' *Basilica* scholia.
[129] See also Stolte, cited earlier, 265.
[130] See also Stolte's remarks in using Byzantine legal sources for the writing of (social) history in Stolte, 'The Social Function of the Law'.

On many occasions, I have been inspired by the writings of historians who have dealt with Byzantine legal sources and have examined issues that combine law and finance, law and literature, law and society; for example, Nicholas Oikonomides, Angeliki Laiou and Ruth Macrides, to mention a few. I hope that in the future, there will be closer co-operation between historians and legal historians who occupy themselves with Byzantine law. Legal history is by definition interdisciplinary,[131] and the treatment of legal sources should not create an obstacle between different disciplines but rather form the ground for fruitful co-operation between them. We have good examples of such a co-operation that we should build on.[132]

Explaining Byzantine law (including Byzantine canon law) and making it more broadly known to a larger audience will prove beneficial for a co-operation between legal historians of Byzantine law and historians who use Byzantine law for other purposes. Publications that can more effectively disseminate the research in the field of Byzantine law are keenly needed. It is therefore fortunate that in the last years, there have been examples of such publications in English including English translations of Byzantine legal sources.[133] We now have a sourcebook on Byzantine law with English translations provided next to the original Greek (and Latin) text[134] and an authoritative handbook.[135] Important and helpful critical editions and translations are being produced.[136] All these books show that there is an interest in Byzantine law. This is also confirmed by two recent monographs, one in German and the other in French which

---

[131] See also here the thoughts of Papadatou, 'Linking Fields, Approaches, and Methods in Byzantine Legal Studies', especially 170.
[132] See Laiou and Simon, *Law and Society in Byzantium*; Caseau and Messis, *Droit et société à Byzance*, and more recently *Subseciva Groningana* XII (2025), which is based on the round table on 'Byzantine studia humanitatis: Bridging disciplines in the 11th and 12th-century Byzantium', which took place at the 24th International Congress of Byzantine Studies in Venice and Padua in 2022.
[133] Chitwood, *Byzantine Legal Culture and the Roman Legal Tradition, 867–1056* (2017), Humphreys, *Law, Power, and Imperial Ideology in the Iconoclast Era, c. 680–850* (2014), Humphreys, *The Laws of the Isaurian Era. The Ecloga and Its Appendices* (2017), Wagschal, *Law and Legality in the Greek East: The Byzantine Canonical Tradition, 381–883* (2015), Miller and Sarris, *The Novels of Justinian: Complete Annotated English Translation* (2018), Morton, *Byzantine Religious Law in Medieval Italy* (2021); see in detail the bibliography at the end of this Element.
[134] Penna and Meijering, *Sourcebook Byzantine law* (2022).
[135] Papagianni and Penna, *Companion Byzantine law* (2025) which consists of twenty-one chapters by sixteen authors.
[136] Simon and Reinsch, Ἡ Πεῖρα – *Die Peira*. This edition is accompanied by a German translation, a commentary and elaborate indices of legal terms, names, and so on.

focus on research on the *Basilica*[137] and a recent French monograph on Byzantine justice.[138] In the field of Byzantine Canon law, there are two recent publications in French.[139]

Now, I come to my last point which is a *desideratum* and refers to the relation between historians of Western medieval law and historians of Byzantine law, something that I have already implied in the previous sections.[140] Nowadays, there is really no dialogue between scholars who study the Western legal tradition and scholars who study the Byzantine legal tradition, with very few exceptions. I argue that a comparative study of the Western and Eastern legal traditions can reveal a lot about the common legal heritage of Europe. The study of Byzantine law is also a study of European law. This is something that most (legal) historians forget. And more generally, the study of Byzantium is not only a study of the History of the Eastern Roman Empire but also a study of European History. It is worth studying Europe's common legal routes and examining how the Western and the Eastern parts of Europe are united in terms of legal history. Perhaps there are more elements that unite Europe than divide it, also in the field of law, and perhaps Byzantine law can play a catalytic role here. In short, I hope I have convinced the reader that Byzantine law, the law of the Eastern Roman Empire, is certainly not boring and can be studied in many ways and for many reasons.

---

[137] De Jong, Ἐντολή *(mandatum) in den Basiliken* (2020) and Giannozzi, *L'homme de bien dans les Basiliques* (2023).

[138] Goudjil, *Une symphonie des pouvoirs judiciaires à Byzance*.

[139] Papathomas (dir.), *Droit canonique et ecclésiastique de l'Église orthodoxe* and Messis, *Le corpus nomocanonique oriental et ses scholiastes du xiie siècle*.

[140] Especially Sections 2.4 and 2.5.

Abbreviations

B.   *Basilicorum libri LX*, ed. Herman J. Scheltema, Douwe Holwerda and Nicolaas van der Wal, Groningen 1953–88.
BS   B., Series B: Scholia (quoted after page and line).
BT   B., Series A: Textus (quoted after page and line).
C.   *Codex Justinianus*, ed. Paul Krüger, *Corpus iuris civilis*, vol. 2, 9th ed., Berlin 1914.
D.   *Digesta*, ed. Theodor Mommsen, *Corpus iuris civilis*, vol. 1, 12th ed., Berlin 1911.
JGR Ioannes Zepos and Panagiotes Zepos, *Jus Graecoromanum*, 8 vols., Athens 1931 (repr. Aalen: 1962).
RhP Georgios Rhalles and Michael Potles, Σύνταγμα τῶν θείων καὶ ἱερῶν κανόνων, 6 vols., Athens 1852–59 (repr. 1966).

Bibliography

Aschenbrenner, Nathanael and Jake Ransohoff, eds. *The Invention of Byzantium in Early Modern Europe*. Dumbarton Oaks, 2021.

Bénou, Lisa. *Pour une nouvelle histoire du droit Byzantin. Théorie et pratique juridiques au XIVe siècle*. Éditions de l'Association Pierre Belon, 2011.

Berman, Harold J. *Law and Revolution: The Formation of the Western Legal Tradition*. Harvard University Press, 1983.

Birks, Peter and Grant McLeod. *Justinian's Institutes with the Latin Text of Paul Kruger*. Duckworth, 1987; repr. 2001.

Brandsma, Frits. 'The Usefulness of the Byzantine Tradition to the Interpretation of the Corpus Iuris Civilis'. In *Introduzione al diritto bizantino, Da Giustiniano ai Basilici*, edited by Johannes H. A. Lokin and Bernard H. Stolte. Pavia University Press, 2011: 681–692.

Burgmann, Ludwig. *Ecloga Basilicorum* (Forschungen zur byzantinischen Rechtsgeschichte, Band 15). Löwenklau-Gesellschaft E.V. Frankfurt, 1998.

Burgmann, Ludwig. 'Vier Richter des 12. Jahrhunderts'. *Jahrbuch der Österreichischen Byzantinistik* 32/2 (1982) (XVI. Internationaler Byzantinisten-Kongreß Wien, 4. – 9. Oktober 1981. Akten II/2): 369–372.

Burgmann, Ludwig and Marie Theres Fögen. 'Florilegium Lesbiacum'. *Fontes Minores* V (1982): 107–178.

Cameron, Averil. *The Byzantines*. Blackwell, 2006.

Cameron, Averil. *Byzantine Matters*. Princeton University Press, 2014.

Cavallo, Guglielmo. *Lire à Byzance*. Les Belles Lettres, 2006.

Chitwood, Zachary. *Byzantine Legal Culture and the Roman Legal Tradition, 867–1056*. Cambridge University Press, 2017.

Codoñer, Signes Juan and Francisco Javier Andrés Santos. *La Introducción al derecho (Eisagoge) del Patriarca Focio*. Madrid, 2007.

De Jong, Hylkje. *Ἐντολή (mandatum) in den Basiliken*. Brill, 2020.

Dimopoulou, Athina. 'Το ρωμαϊκό και βυζαντινορωμαϊκό δίκαιο στη νομολογία των τελευταίων χρόνων' (= *Roman and Byzantine law in jurisprudence of recent years, publication in Greek*). In *Festschrift M.P. Stathopoulos*, Ant. Sakkoula, 2010: 449–464.

Frier, Bruce W. *The Codex of Justinian: A New Annotated Translation with Parallel Latin and Greek Text*. Based on a translation by Justice Fred H. Blume, 3 vols. Cambridge University Press, 2016.

Gallagher, Clarence. 'Gratian and Theodore Balsamon: Two Twelfth-Century Canonistic Methods Compared'. In *Byzantium in the 12th century. Canon Law, State and Society*, edited by Nicholas Oikonomides. Society of Byzantine and Post-Byzantine Studies, 1991: 61–89.

Gastgeber, Christian, Ekaterini Mitsiou, Johannes Preiser-Kapeller and Vratislav Zervan. *A Companion to the Patriarchate of Constantinople*. Brill, 2021.

Gastgeber, Christian, Ekaterini Mitsiou and Johannes Preiser-Kapeller. *The Register of the Patriarchate of Constantinople. An Essential Source for the History and Church of Late Byzantium*. Verlag der Österreichischen Akademie der Wissenschaften, 2013.

Giannozzi, Elena. *L'homme de bien dans les Basiliques*. Mare & Martin, 2023.

Gibbon, Edward. *History of the Decline and Fall of the Roman Empire*. Strahan & Cadell, 1776–1789.

Gordley, James. *The Jurists. A Critical History*. Oxford University Press, 2013.

Goudjil, Romain. *Une symphonie des pouvoirs judiciaires à Byzance. Le rôle de l'Église dans l'administration de la justice (Xe–XVe siècle)*. Sorbonne Université Presses, 2024.

Hallebeek, Jan. 'Structure of Medieval Roman Law: Institutions, Sources, and Methods'. In *The Oxford Handbook of European Legal History*, edited by Heikki Pihlajamäki, Marcus D. Dubber and Marc Godfrey. Oxford University Press, 2018: 286–308.

Heimbach, Gustav E. *Konstantin Harmonopulos. Manuale Legum sive Hexabiblos*. Neudruck der Ausgabe Leipzig, 1851 [repr. Scientia Verlag Aalen, 1969].

Herrin, Judith. *Byzantium, The Surprising Life of a Medieval Empire*. Allen Lane, an imprint of Penguin Books, 2007.

Humphreys, Michael. *The Laws of the Isaurian Era. The Ecloga and Its Appendices*. Liverpool University Press, 2017.

Humphreys, Michael. *Law, Power, and Imperial Ideology in the Iconoclast Era, c. 680–850*. Oxford University Press, 2014.

Iorga, Nicolae. *Byzance après Byzance. Continuation de 'l'histoire de la vie Byzantine'*. Institut d'Etudes Byzantines, 1935.

Kaldellis, Anthony. *Byzantium Unbound*. ARC Humanities Press, 2019.

Kazhdan, Alexander P. 'Do We Need a New History of Byzantine Law?' *Jahrbuch der österreichischen Byzantinistik* 39 (1989): 1–28.

Kermeli, Eugenia. 'The Right to Choice: Ottoman Justice vis-à-vis Ecclesiastical and Communal Justice in the Balkans, Seventeenth-Nineteenth Centuries'. In *Studies in Islamic Law: A Festschrift for Colin Imber*, edited by Andreas Christmann and Robert Gleave. Oxford University Press, 2007: 165–210.

Khalilieh, Hassan S. *Admiralty and Maritime Laws in the Mediterranean Sea (ca. 800–1050). The Kitāb Akriyat al-Sufun vis-à-vis the Nomos Rhodion Nautikos*. Brill, 2006.

Kotzageorgis, Phokion. 'Δικαιϊκός πλουραλισμός (legal pluralism) στην οθωμανική αυτοκρατορία: Οι χριστιανοί στα οθωμανικά και εκκλησιαστικά δικαστήρια πριν το Τανζιμάτ'. [= Legal pluralism in the Ottoman Empire: Christians in the Ottoman and Ecclesiastical Courts before the Tanzimat]. In Βαλκανικά Σύμμεικτα [ΙΜΧΑ], 18 (2017): 8–28.

Laiou, Angeliki E. and Dieter Simon. *Law and Society in Byzantium, Ninth–Twelfth Centuries*. Harvard University Press, 1994.

Liebs, Detlef. 'Roman Vulgar Law in Late Antiquity'. In *Aspects of Law in Late Antiquity. Dedicated to A.M. Honoré on the Occasion of the Sixtieth Year of His Teaching in Oxford*, edited by Boudewijn Sirks. All Sourls College: 35–53.

Lokin, Johannes H. A., Roos Meijering, Berharnd H. Stolte and Nicolaas van der Wal. *Theophili Antecessoris Paraphrasis Institutionum*, with a translation by A. F. Murison. Chimaira, 2010.

Macrides, Ruth. 'The Competent Court'. In *Law and Society in Byzantium: Ninth – Twelfth Centuries*, edited by Angeliki E. Laiou and Dieter Simon. Dumbarton Oaks Research Library and Collection, 1994: 117–129.

Macrides, Ruth. 'Perception of the Past in the Twelfth-Century Canonists'. In *Byzantium in the 12th Century: Canon Law, State and Society*, edited by Nicholas Oikonomides. Etaireia Byzantinon kai Metabyzantinon Meleton 'Diptykon' Paraphylla 3, 1991 Athens 1991 (repr. in *Ruth Macrides, Kinship and Justice in Byzantium, 11th–15th Centuries*, Ashgate Variorum 1999, VII).

Magdalino, Paul. 'The Maritime Neighborhoods of Constantinople: Commercial and Residential Functions, Sixth to Twelfth Centuries'. *Dumbarton Oaks Papers* 54 (2000): 209–227 [repr. in P. Magdalino, *Studies on the History and Topography of Byzantine Constantinople*, Aldershot 2007].

Maner, Hans-Christian. '"Byzance après Byzance" –Nicolae Iorga's Concept and Its Aftermath'. In *Imagining Byzantium. Perceptions, Patterns, Problems*, edited by Alena Alshanskaya, Andreas Gietzen and Christina Hadjiafxenti. (Byzanz zwischen Orient und Okzident, Band 11), Verl. d. Römisch-Germanischen Zentralmuseums, 2018: 31–38. Available also online: https://doi.org/10.11588/propylaeum.703.

Markopoulos, Athanasios. 'Education'. In *The Oxford Handbook of Byzantine Studies*, edited by Elizabeth Jeffreys with John Haldon and Robin Cormack. Oxford University Press, 2008: 785–795.

Markopoulos, Athanasios. 'Education in Constantinople during the Byzantine Period'. Available online: https://istanbultarihi.ist/651-education-in-constantinople-during-the-byzantine-period.

Matses, Nikolaos P. 'Τὰ σχόλια εἰς τὴν Ἑξάβιβλον τοῦ Ἁρμενοπούλου καὶ ἡ Ἐκλογή ἐκ τῶν 10 πρώτων βιβλίων τῶν Βασιλικῶν'. [= The scholia to the *Hexabiblos* of Harmenopoulos and the *Ecloga* of the first 10 books of the *Basilica*]. *Byzantinisch-Neugriechische Jahrbücher* 21 (1971–74 [1976]): 169–176.

Messis, Charis. *Le corpus nomocanonique oriental et ses scholiastes du xiie siècle : les commentaires sur le concile in Trullo*, 691–692. Centre d'études byzantines, néo-helléniques et sud-est européennes, École des hautes études en sciences sociales, CéSor (Dossiers byzantins, 18/1), 2020.

Miller, David and Peter Sarris. *The Novels of Justinian: Complete Annotated English Translation*. Cambridge University Press, 2018.

Montesquieu. *Considérations sur les causes de la grandeur des Romains et de leur decadence*. Jacques Desbordes, 1734.

Morton, James. *Byzantine Religious Law in Medieval Italy*. Oxford University Press, 2021.

Neville, Leonora. *Sailing Away from Byzantium toward East Roman History*. Cambridge University Press, 2025.

Oikonomides, Nicolas. 'The "Peira" of Eustathios Rhomaios: An Abortive Attempt to Innovate in Byzantine Law'. *Fontes Minores* VII (1986), 169–192 (= Nicolas Oikonomides, Byzantium from the Ninth Century to the Fourth Crusade. Studies, Texts, Monuments, no. XII, Aldershot, 1992).

Pahlitzsch, Johannes. *Der arabische Procheiros Nomos. Untersuchung und Edition der arabischen Übersetzung eines byzantinischen Rechtstextes*. Lowenklau-Gesellschaft E.V., 2014.

Pantazopoulos, Nikolaos J. *Church and Law in the Balkan Peninsula during the Ottoman Rule*. Institute for Balkan Studies, 1967.

Papadatou, Daphne. 'Linking Fields, Approaches, and Methods in Byzantine Legal Studies'. In *Proceedings of the 24th International Congress of Byzantine Studies Plenary Sessions*, edited by Emiliano Fiori and Michele Trizio. Edizioni Ca'. Foscari, 2022.

Papagianni, Eleftheria. 'Το διαζύγιο στο Βυζάντιο: Κοινωνικές αντιλήψεις, νομοθετική πολιτική και εκκλησιαστική πρακτική' [= Divorce in Byzantine law, publication in Greek]. In *Volume in memoriam Th. K. Papachristou*. Ant. Sakkoula, 2019: 1351–1374.

Papagianni, Eleftheria. '4.2. Canon Law and Its Status in the Byzantine Legal System'. In *Brill's New Pauly Supplements II*

Online – Volume 10. Brill, 2018. https://doi-org.proxy-ub.rug.nl/10.1163/2468-3418_bnps10_COM_200358.

Papagianni, Eleftheria. '4.4 Courts and Justice'. In *Brill's New Pauly Supplements II Online* – Volume 10. Brill, 2018. https://doi-org.proxy-ub.rug.nl/10.1163/2468-3418_bnps10_COM_200618.

Papagianni, Eleftheria. Η νομολογία των εκκλησιαστικών δικαστηρίων της βυζαντινής και μεταβυζαντινής περιόδου σε θέματα περιουσιακού δικαίου [= The Jurisprudence of the Ecclesiastical Courts of Byzantine and post-Byzantine Period in Matters of Property Law, 3 vols., publications in Greek]. Ant. N. Sakkoula, 1992, 1997 and 2010.

Papagianni, Eleftheria and Daphne Penna, eds. *From the Foundation of Constantinople (330) until the End of the Macedonian Dynasty (1056)*. Brill, 2025.

Papaioannou, Stratis. *Michael Psellus Epistulae*, ed. vol. 1. De Gruyter, 2019.

Paparriga-Artemiades, Lydia. 'Les scoliastes byzantins face aux ambiguïtés des lois'. *Revue des Études Byzantines* 77 (2019): 225–256.

Paparriga-Artemiades, Lydia. 'Interventions of the *interpretatio iuris* to the Resolving of the Ambiguities of Law during the Byzantine Period'. *Humanitas* 69 (2017): 81–109.

Papathomas, Grigorios D. (dir.). *Droit canonique et ecclésiastique de l'Église orthodoxe. Sources, histoire, institutions et particularités*. Strasbourg, Presses universitaires, 2024.

Penna, Daphne. 'Justice in Byzantium: Blind or Biased?' In *Byzantine Justice. Society for the Promotion of Byzantine Studies*, edited by Anne Alwis and Laura Franco. Routledge, in press.

Penna, Daphne. 'Law Teaching at the Time of Justinian'. In *A Companion to Byzantine Law. From the Foundation of Constantinople (330) until the End of the Macedonian Dynasty (1056)*, edited by Eleftheria Papagianni and Daphne Penna. Brill, 2025: 134–153.

Penna, Daphne. 'Classical Literature in Byzantine Legal Sources'. *Subseciva Groningana* XII (2025): 111–131.

Penna, Daphne. 'Studying the 'new' *Basilica* scholia: A First Evaluation'. In *Byzantinische Rechtsgeschichte im internationalen Kontext. Akten einer Tagung der Akademien der Wissenschaften zu Göttingen und Sofia (28.9.–1.10.2021)*, edited by Peter Schreiner, Jens Peter Laut, Ivan Biliarsky in collaboration with Isabel Grimm-Stadelmann. De Gruyter 2024: 131–141.

Penna, Daphne. 'Hagiotheodorites, Once again. A Few Remarks on Two of His *Basilica* scholia'. *Yearbook of the Research Centre for the History of Greek Law* 51 (2022): 329–344.

Penna, Daphne. 'Religious Influences on Medieval Civil Law, The *pacta sunt servanda* principle in Byzantine and Medieval Western Law'. In *Droit et société à Byzance et dans sa sphère d'influence* [Actes du colloque international Droit et société au Moyen Âge, Maison de la recherche de la Sorbonne Université 12 et 13 septembre 2019], edited by Béatrice Caseau and Charis Messis, Dossiers byzantins 21, Centre d'études byzantines, néo-helléniques et sud-est euraopéennes, César, UMR 8216, EHESS, CNRS, 2022: 33–50.

Penna, Daphne. 'The Eleventh-Century Byzantine Jurist Nicaeus: His Scholia on the Basilica Laws and His Connection to the *Meditatio de nudis*'. *Fontes Minores* XIII (2021): 111–131.

Penna, Daphne. 'Of the Nomophylax: John Xiphilinos' scholia on the *Basilica*'. *Byzantinische Zeitschrift* 114/3 (2021): 1263–1302.

Penna, Daphne. 'A Witness of Byzantine Legal Practice in the Twelfth Century. Some Remarks on the Construction of the *Ecloga Basilicorum*'. *Subseciva Groningana* X (2019): 139–162.

Penna, Daphne. 'Similar Problems, Similar Solutions? Byzantine Chrysobulls and Crusader Charters on Legal Issues Regarding the Italian Maritime Republics'. In *Byzantium in Dialogue with the Mediterranean: History and Heritage*, edited by Daniëlle Slootjes and Mariëtte Verhoeven. Brill, 2019: 162–181.

Penna, Daphne. 'Odd Topics, Old Methods and the Cradle of the Ius Commune: Byzantine Law and the Italian City-States'. *Utrecht Law Review* 13/3 (2017): 49–55.

Penna, Daphne. 'Piracy and Reprisal in Byzantine Waters: Resolving a Maritime Conflict between Byzantines and Genoese at the End of the Twelfth Century'. *Comparative Legal History* 5/1 (2017): 36–52.

Penna, Daphne. 'Hagiotheodorites: The Last Antecessor? Some Remarks on One of the "new" *Basilica* scholiasts'. *Subseciva Groningana* IX (2014): 399–427.

Penna, Daphne. *The Byzantine Imperial Acts to Venice, Pisa and Genoa, 10th–12th Centuries. A Comparative Legal Study*. Eleven International Publishing, 2012.

Penna, Daphne and Roos Meijering. *A Sourcebook on Byzantine Law. Illustrating Byzantine Law through the Sources*. Brill, 2022.

Pennington, Kenneth. 'The "Big Bang": Roman Law in the Early Twelfth Century'. *Rivista internationale di diritto comune* 18 (2007): 43–70.

Pitsakis, Constantine. "Ἡ ἱστορία τῆς Ῥώμης καὶ τοῦ ῥωμαϊκοῦ δικαίου στὰ βυζαντινὰ καὶ μεταβυζαντινὰ νομικὰ ἐγχειρίδια', in Greek (= The History of Rome and of Roman law in Byzantine and Post-Byzantine legal manuals). In Τιμαὶ Ἰωάννου Τριανταφυλλόπουλου (= Festschrift I. Triantaphyllopoulos), edited by Julia Velissaropoulou-Karakosta, Spyros Troianos, Kalliopi Bourdara, Michael Stathopoulos and Nikolaos Klamares. Ant. N. Sakkoula, 2000: 399–436.

Pitsakis, Constantine. *Κωνσταντίνου Ἁρμενοπούλου, Πρόχειρον Νόμων ἢ Ἑξάβιβλος*. Dodoni, 1971.

Prinzing, Günter. *Demetrios Chomatenos, Ponemata diaphora. Das Aktenkorpus des Ohrider Erzbischofs Demetrios Chomatenos. Einleitung, kritische Edition und Indizes*. De Gruyter, 2002.

Racine, Jean. *Les Plaideurs*, C. Barbin, 1669.

Rhalles Georgios, A. and Michael Potles. *Σύνταγμα τῶν θείων καὶ ἱερῶν κανόνων*, 6 vols. G. Chartophylax, 1852–59 (repr. 1966).

Runciman, Steven. 'Gibbon and Byzantium'. *Daedalus*, Summer, 1976, vol. 105, No. 3.

Saradi, Helen. 'The Byzantine Tribunals: Problems in the Application of Justice and State Policy (9th–12th c.)'. *Revue des études byzantines* 53 (1995): 165–204.

Sarris, Peter. *Justinian: Emperor, Soldier, Saint*. Basic Books, 2023.

Scheltema, Herman J., Douwe Hokwerda and Nicolaas van der Wal, (eds). *Basilicorum libri LX*. Groningen, 1953–88.

Scheltema, Herman J. *L'enseignement de droit des antécesseurs*. Brill 1970 [repr. in *H.J. Scheltema, Opera Minora ad iuris historiam pertinentia*, collegerunt N. van der Wal, J. H. A. Lokin, B. H. Stolte, R. Meijering, A3: 58-110, Chimaira 2004].

Simon, Dieter. *Rechtsfindung am byzantinischen Reichsgericht*. V. Klostermann, 1973 [reprinted and updated in Dieter Simon, *Rechtshistorische Schriften. Antike und Mittelalter*, herausgegeben von Silvia Neye, De Gruyter 2025, Band 1, 297–312, no 10].

Simon, Dieter. 'Byzantinische Provinzialjustiz'. *Byzantinische Zeitschrift* 79 (1986): 310–343 [reprinted and updated in Dieter Simon, *Rechtshistorische Schriften. Antike und Mittelalter*, herausgegeben von Silvia Neye, De Gruyter 2025, Band 2, 991–1034, no 39].

Simon, Dieter and Diether R. Reinsch. *Ἡ Πεῖρα – Die Peira. Ein juristisches Lehrbuch des 11. Jahrhunderts aus Konstantinopel – Text, Übersetzung, Kommentar, Glossar*. De Gruyter, 2022.

Sirks, Boudewijn. 'How Legal Is the Peira? Cases and Problems'. 2012. Retrieved from https://ora.ox.ac.uk/objects/uuid:5a059028-3045-4956-95f3-b598f06337a/files/mf3764df67b198932cb5e27701f60e074

Sirks, Boudewijn. 'Peira 45.11, a presumed succession pact, and the Peira as legal source'. In *Quellen zur byzantinischen Rechtspraxis. Aspekte der*

Textüberlieferung, Paläographie und Diplomatik: Akten des internationalen Symposiums, Wien, 5.–7.11.2007, edited by Christian Gastgeber. Verlag der Österreichischen Akademie der Wissenschaften, 2010: 189–199.

Sirks, Boudewijn. 'The Peira: Roman Law in Greek Setting'. In *Studi in onore di Remo Martini*, vol. III. edited by Giuffrè editore, 2009: 583–591.

Stein, Peter. *Roman Law in European History*. Cambridge University Press, 2002.

Stolte, Bernard H. 'Byzantine Law: The Law of the New Rome'. In *The Oxford Handbook of European Legal History*, edited by Heikki Pihlajamaki, Markus D. Dubber and Mark Godfrey. Oxford University Press, 2018: 229–248.

Stolte, Bernard H. 'The Law of New Rome: Byzantine Law'. In *The Cambridge Companion to Roman Law*, edited by David Johnston. Cambridge University Press, 2015: 355–373.

Stolte, Bernard H. 'The Social Function of the Law'. In *The Social History of Byzantium*, edited by John Haldon. Blackwell Publishing, 2009: 76–91.

Stolte, Bernard H. 'Is Byzantine Law Roman Law?' *Acta Byzantina Fennica Ser. NS* 2 (2003/04): 111–126.

Stolte, Bernard H. 'Not New but Novel. Notes on the Historiography of Byzantine Law'. *Byzantine and Modern Greek Studies* 22 (1998): 264–279.

Tantalos, Marios, Th. 'The History of Research on Byzantine Law'. In *A Companion to Byzantine Law*, edited by Eleftheria Papagianni and Daphne Penna. Brill, 2025: 33–42.

Tantalos, Marios, Th. 'Forms of Suretyship in the *Peira* in the Light of the *Basilica*'. *Tijdschrift voor Rechtsgeschiedenis* 89/1–2 (2021): 93–124. Available also online https://doi.org/10.1163/15718190-12340004.

Tantalos, Marios, Th. 'Τὰ «Βασιλικὰ Ἰνστιτοῦτα» (1706). Ἕνα ἀθησαύριστο ἔργο τοῦ Νικολάου Κομνηνοῦ Παπαδοπούλου καὶ ἡ διάδοσή του στὸν ἑλληνικὸ χῶρο' (= The «Royal Institutes» (1706). An Unknown Work of Nikolaos Komnenos Papadopoulos and its Diffusion, publication in Greek). *The Gleaner/ Ο Ερανιστής/* 28 (2011), In Memoriam of C. G. Patrinelis: 141–159.

Taubenschlag, Rafał. *The Law of Greco-Roman Egypt in the Light of the papyri, 332 B.C.–640 A.D.* Warszawa: Państwowe Wydawnictwo Naukowe, 1955.

Troianos, Spyros. 'The Creation of a Parallel Legal Order: Canon Law'. In *A Companion to Byzantine Law. From the Foundation of Constantinople (330) until the End of the Macedonian Dynasty (1056)*, edited by Eleftheria Papagianni and Daphne Penna. Brill, 2025: 16–32.

Troianos, Spyros. *Die Quellen des byzantinischen Rechts*, translated by Dieter Simon and Sylvia Neye. De Gruyter, 2017.

Troianos, Spyros. *Οι Νεαρές του Λέοντος ς' του Σοφού (= The Novels of Leo VI the Wise, publication in Greek)*. Herodotos, 2007.

Troianos, Spyros. *Η ελληνική νομική γλώσσα. Γένεση και μορφολογική εξέλιξη της νομικής ορολογίας στη ρωμαϊκή Ανατολή (= The Greek legal language. Genesis and morphological evolution of legal terminology in the Roman East, publication in Greek)*, Ant. N. Sakkoula, 2000.

Van Bochove, Thomas E. 'Some Byzantine Law Books. Introducing the Continuous Debate Concerning their Status and their Date'. In *Introduzione al diritto bizantino, Da Giustiniano ai Basilici*, edited by Johannes H. A. Lokin and Bernard H. Stolte. Pavia University Press, 2011: 239–266.

Van der Wal, Nicolaas. 'Les termes techniques grecs dans la langue des juristes byzantins'. *Subseciva Groningana* VI (1999): 127–141.

Van der Wal, Nicolaas. 'Die Schreibweise der dem Lateinischen entlehnten Fachworte in der frühbyzantinischen Juristensprache'. *Scriptorium* 37 (1983): 29–53.

Vinogradoff, Paul. *Roman Law in Medieval Europe*. Harper & Brothers, 1909.

Voltaire. *Le Pyrrhonisme de l'histoire*. Garnier, 1879. Retrieved 22/02/2025 from: https://fr.wikisource.org/wiki/Le_Pyrrhonisme_de_l%E2%80%99histoire/%C3%89ditionGarnier/15.

Wagschal, David. *Law and Legality in the Greek East: The Byzantine Canonical Tradition, 381–883*. Oxford University Press, 2015.

Yiftach, Uri. 'Law in Graeco-Roman Egypt: Hellenization, Fusion, Romanization'. In *The Oxford Handbook of Papyrology*, edited by Roger S. Bagnall. Oxford University Press, 2011: 541–560.

Zepos, Ioannes and Panagiotes Zepos. *Jus Graecoromanum*, 8 vols. G. Fexis, 1931 (repr. Aalen: 1962).

Zimmermann, Reinhard. *The Law of Obligations. Roman Foundations of the Civilian Tradition*. Oxford University Press, 1996.

About the Author

Daphne Penna is Assistant Professor of Legal History at the University of Groningen and Associate Professor of Roman Law at KU Leuven. She has published extensively on Roman and Byzantine law, and especially on their influence on the European legal tradition.

Cambridge Elements

Rethinking Byzantium

Leonora Neville
University of Wisconsin-Madison

Leonora Neville is the John and Jeanne Rowe Professor of Byzantine History and Vilas Distinguished Achievement Professor at the University of Wisconsin-Madison. She has written extensively on eastern Roman society, particularly on authority in provincial communities, history writing, gender, and the importance of the classical past for medieval Roman culture.

Darlene Brooks Hedstrom
Brandeis University

Darlene Brooks Hedstrom is the Myra and Robert Kraft and Jacob Hiatt Chair in Christian Studies at Brandeis University. She is an archaeologist and historian of the late antique Mediterranean world. Her works examine the intersection of objects, religious practice, monasticism, and the history of archaeology.

About the Series

Elements in Rethinking Byzantium offer crisp and accessible introductions to vibrant current research on medieval eastern Roman society and culture which sets them within broader schemas of pre-modern history and cultural study. Individual Elements address various aspects of visual and literary cultures, history, and religion in the territory and cultural sphere of the Roman Empire, broadly conceived, from the fourth to fifteenth centuries CE.

Cambridge Elements⁼

Rethinking Byzantium

Elements in the Series

Kyivan Rus in Medieval Europe
Christian Raffensperger

Sailing Away from Byzantium Toward East Roman History
Leonora Neville

Byzantine Law: The Law of the Eastern Roman Empire
Daphne Penna

A full series listing is available at: www.cambridge.org/RTHB

For EU product safety concerns, contact us at Calle de José Abascal, 56–1°,
28003 Madrid, Spain or eugpsr@cambridge.org.

www.ingramcontent.com/pod-product-compliance
Lightning Source LLC
LaVergne TN
LVHW011858060526
838200LV00054B/4408